SHADOW

How meth-driven crime is eating at the heart of rural America

PEOPLE

SCOTT THOMAS ANDERSON

Coalition for Investigative Journalism

Library of Congress Control Number: 2011961644
ISBN: 978-0-615-55191-3

For inquires about volume orders, please contact editorial coordinator:
The Coalition for Investigative Journalism
Email: C.J.Journalism@live.com
Mail inquires:
Coalition for Investigative Journalism
P.O. Box 1553
Folsom, CA 95763-1553

The Coalition for Investigative Journalism is a club for professional and free-lance reporters who are trying to preserve the critically wounded art of investigative journalism. For
more information visit: cijournalism.com

The production of this book was made possible in part by research funding from the Phillips Foundation, a 501(c)(3) nonprofit group in Washington D.C., advisory support by
Manzanita Writers Press, a nonprofit publishing house in California and private financial
donations by citizens using Kickstarter.com, a website for following and funding the Arts.

This book was written with the assistance of four professional journalistic editors and one
professional scientific editor. The book was produced with editorial coordination from the
Coalition for Investigative Journalism, a national club based in California.

Designed and printed in the United States of America

"The infernal hurricane that never rests,
hurtles the spirits before its violence"

— Dante Alighieri
The Divine Comedy: Hell

CHAPTER 1

Jackson, California: May 19

THE DISTRICT ATTORNEY still sees the face of Grover Graham. It's a Wednesday afternoon and Todd Riebe is the only man wearing a suit in a poorly lit sports bar north of Jackson. He sits near the window, his glasses hit by an alabaster light off the flat screen televisions and pale fuchsia twinkle from the old Budweiser logo. A grill hisses with smoke. The waitress elbows past a bridge of construction workers, until she slips under inflatable Coronas, NFL banners and a life-sized hammerhead shark swimming through the crooked ceiling fans. Riebe looks down at the burger she drops in front of him. He tries to say thank you, but the newspaper reporter cuts him off. "What can you tell me about the Callahan case?" Riebe hears from across the table. He hesitates. Victor Callahan is a defendant his office is going at hard, preparing to charge the fifty-two-year-old with second-degree murder, vehicular manslaughter and a special allegation of inflicting great bodily injury on an elderly person. Riebe's certain that blood evidence will prove Callahan committed every offense while his brain was heated in a strobe-glow of methamphetamine. The district attorney remains quiet as he looks out the window. The name murmured over the spitting grease may belong to Victor Callahan; but, for Riebe, it's Grover Graham's eyes that flicker out of the shadows.

On March 31, 1994, a dented Ford Granada sped past the fields of Merced, cutting through the warm, soil-swept farmlands of central California. It hugged along ragged weeds, a littered roadside, dry oats and gutter dust, until it approached a cumulus of almond trees beyond Chowchilla. Maria Graham kept her hands on the steering wheel and looked over to her husband of seven years, Grover. Maria understood that Grover was hearing voices. She knew he was watching freakish faces twitch at him from the glass of passing windows. At times she caught his eyes drifting in shocked terror into the sky, as he appeared to track something that hovered just between his consciousness and the coiling black spots on the sun. Grover kept the couple's four-month-old daughter, Candice, trapped in his arms. He held her tight. He muttered nervously above the child's ear. He remained paralyzed by the quick, blurred jackal glances from diesel trucks overhead. Maria suddenly turned to her husband and begged, "Please don't hurt my baby!" And then she started to pray.

In the days leading up to her prayer on the highway, Maria watched Grover plummet into a dithered "crank" binge. Slowly and steadily, he became unnerved by his methamphetamine use. A chemically conjured world of menacing profiles began to strangle his thoughts, to tighten down on his existence. Grover responded by spending the next five days putting only meth and diet coke into his body.

On the morning of March 31, Maria headed out to her job at a fast food diner in Hilmar. It was her family's main source of income. The day was clear. Cloudless. Grover soon phoned her in a panic, rambling about sinister men conspiring to kill him for a life insurance policy that Maria knew did not exist. Across the lines of the receiver, she could hear Candice wailing. Maria came home to find Grover crying with Candice fast in his arms, sputtering the warning, "they're going to kill me." He told Maria that he'd set up a "defensive perimeter" around the house, which she recognized as a fragile psychic echo of his brief stint in the military. Trembling, Grover inched to the window as he wielded a long, cooking knife in one hand and Candice in the other. "This is my protection," he told his wife. "My protection."

It was midmorning by the time Maria talked Grover into putting down the knife. Surrendering his blade was one thing, but letting go of Candice was different. Grover kept the tiny baby held firmly against his chest. By 11 a.m. Maria convinced her husband to turn himself into the Fresno Veterans Hospital for emergency psychiatric treatment. It was a glimmer of hope for the family; but even heading out to the car, Grover's head was penetrated by a phantom litany of voices whispering about his death. He stopped to grab a pair of scissors.

On Highway 99, Grover continued to hold Candice in his arms. Out the window, bleached, bent faces started to watch him from passing trucks. "It's a sniper!" Grover yelled. The faces came again, and Grover panted "sniper" each time a contorted expression gazed on him from the high, sun-touched windshields. Grover was becoming increasingly agitated and Maria began to speak to God. Grover looked up to see what he would later call "sky skins" — floating carpets of disembodied flesh slowly tumbling across the sky. Maria kept driving, kept praying, kept waiting for the long, crowded freeway to take her to the next city ahead. Without warning, Grover turned to her, believing that the face of his wife had just fluttered into a boar's head dripping with blood. "Now is when we all die," Grover said. He raised his scissors up.

ROBERT LEWIS. The quintessential trucker. A big man who loved commanding eighteen wheels under steel and the growl of a 400-horsepower engine. Lewis was known as a genial twenty-five-year veteran of the freeways, a man who could never resist pulling over to help a stranded motorist as he moved down a boundless agricultural thoroughfare. For Lewis, March 31, 1994, started like any other day along the concrete river. He was hauling a load of produce north on Highway 99, every mile taking him farther away from his children, a grandchild and his wife, Jennie. At 11:10 a.m., as Lewis's truck charged past the off-ramp for Chowchilla, he noticed dust rising around a Ford parked in the weeds. Lewis turned his eyes from the south shoulder to the median and witnessed a fast, flailing tangle of limbs, and then the outline of a man on top of a woman, driving his fists into the back of her cranium.

Lewis hit his brakes.

At the same moment that Robert Lewis jumped down from his eighteen-wheeler, another trucker, Andrew Griffith, was heading northbound on the freeway. Griffith knew something was wrong and swerved for the median. In the few seconds it took him to stop, a violent mirage passed under his air brakes: A salivating man straddling a woman, hammering her with punches, wrenching her head through the gravel and grit as he tried to force it under speeding cars.

Lewis reached them first. Maria was covered in blood as Grover's knuckles batted her skull up and down against the pavement. Though Lewis had recently suffered a heart attack, he instantly lunged at Grover. It was a brutal struggle. The trucker outweighed the other man, but he was fighting against a homicidal adrenalin—a quaking rage amplified by the stimulant coursing through his opponent's blood. And Grover foamed. He thrashed against the rough, deranged faces blowing in the dirt around him. Lewis eventually managed to knock Grover away from Maria. Fueled by meth, Grover went wild, flopping around and blathering incoherently.

Griffith rushed over to help. It was then the heart-stopping words came, Maria calling up from the ground, "My baby!" The pair of scissors had fallen on the roadside—stained, red instruments that were dropped after Grover pursued Maria out of the car, across traffic and into the median. Now Maria looked up, begging, "Please go check on my baby!"

Horrified by the chaos erupting out on the freeway, John Ashby, of Modesto, had also pulled over. He would later break down in tears in front of a judge describing what he'd witnessed that day: Maria screaming in the bushes, Grover rolling and ranting in the median, the stunned truck drivers; and a young, off-duty paramedic cradling a limp infant girl in his arms, gently doing chest compressions.

IN 1994, Todd Riebe wasn't Amador County's district attorney, he was one of Madera County's top public defenders. A public defender is a special breed of legal combatant. Appointed by the court to represent those accused of everything from dishonesty to brutality—sometimes depravity—public defenders sleep at night by focusing on America's protected rights and freedoms. Sometimes they inherit clients who are innocent.

More often they meet clients whose criminal charges are debatable. And, sometimes, a public defender represents a client who makes the average stomach fall, or the ordinary spine throw a tremor. In these instances, many public defenders see themselves not so much fighting for the accused as they are fighting for the United States Constitution. This was the star Riebe followed in 1994, and yet no legal philosophy could make his task any easier the day the Chowchilla Justice Court appointed him to represent Grover Lee Graham, a man accused of stabbing his little, four-month-old daughter to death with a pair of scissors.

On the afternoon details of Candice's slaying first echoed through court, a newspaper photographer captured Grover and Riebe together: Grover looking on blankly, a finger hung from his jaw, and Riebe at his shoulder, clad in a dark suit and power tie, sandy-blond hair combed up, eyes turning behind his glasses with a stern, cautious intensity, away from his client and toward the prosecutors.

Robert Lewis, Andrew Griffith and John Ashby all took the stand; but it was Maria's testimony that was the most piercing. With Judge David Minier by her side, Maria recalled how she had begged Grover, "Please don't kill my baby," and then how she'd begged God above "for nothing to happen."

These were words that would gnaw though the minds of any jury. Riebe knew it. They preyed on his thoughts as well. Maria's testimony raised an inescapable question: Prior to that day in March, Grover had never been violent toward her or Candice. Given the level of methamphetamine in Grover's blood and hallucinations he'd experienced during the attack, Riebe turned to mental health professionals. Two doctors concluded that Grover had suffered from "Amphetamine-induced

Psychotic Disorder with delusions" at the time of his offenses. Riebe believed that simply providing Judge Minier with the facts of the case—Grover's whispering snipers, the floating sky skins, the gruesome boar's muzzle splashed in blood—would be enough to prove that meth had literally driven his client mad. Madera County prosecutors looked at the chilling evidence and found little argument with Grover's diagnosis. On October 31, Riebe stood at Grover's side as he pleaded guilty but not guilty by reason of insanity to one count of murder and one count of attempted murder. The judge had Grover booked into Napa State Hospital, with the potential to serve a maximum commitment of life. Grover tearfully hugged Riebe before sheriff's deputies led him away.

The construction workers at the bar suddenly grow loud, forcing Riebe to look down at the half-eaten remnants of his hamburger. So, what's changed in sixteen years? Just a month ago, the region's largest newspaper ran a story about Danny Ray Poplin Jr., a deaf man who was convicted of running a 13-inch butcher knife through the stomach of his pregnant girlfriend while ramped on methamphetamine. Poplin was handed fifty-years-to-life for fetal homicide.

Riebe glances out the window toward the head frame of an abandoned mine, a weathered iron trachea above chimneys, brome and the low saffron hills. His legal jurisdiction sits at the very heart of the California Gold Country. It's a place where strangers are captivated by majestic views—by the gentle oceans of vines, the sun-baked gravel roads, the cypress trees and goat pastures, the smooth terra cotta roofs set on reams of blue-bell sky. Olive trees cover the landscape in brushy mint fountains, like half-wild patches of history itself, leaning out, twisting up and fanning across the hills with branches of small, speckled fruit that gleam in the afternoon sun. Past legacies are cherished here, and the region is famous for its little western towns and rolling vistas dotted with mining wheels and old Chinese gambling halls. Most cattle ranches and orchards are still owned by the same families that broke the range during the glitter boom of 1849.

But Todd Riebe understands better than anyone that there's also a different face to these hills. Or, better put, there are different faces—cadaverous faces wrecked with blisters, scabs and open sores; faces permanently disfigured by rotting teeth and emaciated skin. Riebe has memorized the eroded jaws, the collapsed nasal tents. He's aware of what the pocked heads mean and everything that comes with them. In the twelve years he's been district attorney, he's seen methamphetamine-related crimes soar throughout his stretch of California. The county probation department ran an internal study several months ago that determined in the last four years 50 percent of its felony offenders admitted to methamphetamine addiction or had a known history of meth use. The anecdotal evidence is over. There's finally a hard number to prove what Riebe and every cop and social worker in the area already knows—that methamphetamine is rearing its head behind a paralyzing array of felonies that includes burglary, robbery, larceny, spousal battery, child abuse, financial elder abuse, physical elder abuse, sexual assault, public assault, identity theft, fraud, mail theft and, most notably this year, vehicular manslaughter. Riebe fights it all partly with a handful of investigators who answer directly to him; and there's little they haven't seen now. Dirty children covered in flea bites? His men have led them out of the houses. Six-year-old boys whose teeth are eaten with holes from exposure to the fumes of their parents' meth labs. Riebe's investigators have watched them driven off to the hospitals. For Riebe it's been one hundred and forty-one months of prosecuting meth addicts for nearly every crime in the state's penal code. He has sat through their trials. He's watched the robotic issuance of prison terms. In more cases than he cares to remember, he has witnessed the same faces dragged through the same courtroom again. So many faces. Today, the face the reporter is asking about belongs to Victor Callahan. But, when it comes to images of blood and tragedy on a roadside—or the true, naked horror of methamphetamine—for Riebe, it's Grover Graham who waits in the darkest corner.

Grover Graham saw shadow people. The term refers to hallucinogenic figures glimpsed by methamphetamine addicts after days without sleep. But in reality it's the addicts themselves who are living in a shadow, growing in numbers, becoming an alarming subculture on the periphery of rural America, engaging in crimes that are having devastating impact on places where traditional life is valued most. It touches the California Gold Country, even as families venture through summer fairs, walking in drifts of barbecue smoke, carnival lights and the strangely intoxicating fragrance of cheap beer over steer manure. Meth touches the broken, red-capped hills of eastern Montana, where train whistles growl on iron bridges, ricocheting along the facades of the lasting frontier settlements, where hunters bond with the cooked grass and elk trails, where stock growers drive their cattle across a hell-tinted steppe that runs to the very end of the horizon. Meth touches the fields of Iowa and Nebraska and the lives of men hauling chisel plows through slow erupting soil, until the sun fires clouds like shining wheat, until high school gymnasiums fill with screaming parents, until pickup trucks sail under water towers basked in the gorgeous light of a dying afternoon. It touches the rows of apartments and mobile homes in northern Georgia, from the seam of the Chattahooche National Forest to Calhoun, the city where a hardware store leaves its items out overnight without chains, where the Sunday morning sound of church bells can be heard around every brick corner, where "Support our Troops" signs jut proudly up from chic, southern gardens. Meth touches countless shades of the rural dream. Those who live on the original outlands and search for inspiration in the country's past feel its kaiser blade through felonies, through ongoing acts that continue to eviscerate their communities, cutting them apart, one piece at a time.

CHAPTER 2
Shadows on the Silos

IT WAS A TALE that would echo in halls of the Saunders County Sheriff's Office: In February 2010, a methamphetamine addict was arrested for burglarizing farmhouses across the lower Platte Valley in eastern Nebraska. He had stolen nearly $10,000 in property between three victims. He was looking at a host of felony charges. His bail was higher than what some locals make in a year. On the third week of March, the addict appeared before Judge Marvin Miller and was granted a conditional release from custody on bond, pending his trial. He walked out of the judge's presence, was passed a small object in the hallway, went through another set of doors and—inside the men's room of the Saunders County Courthouse—proceeded to snort a long, white rail of methamphetamine.

Outside, a line of American flags tussled under the belly of a torpedo, the monument to a Pacific prowler that sank twenty Japanese ships before it was blown to its watery end in 1943. That submarine, the U.S.S. Wahoo, shared its name with the capital of Saunders County. The addict walked out of the new justice center, moving by the sun-blinding torpedo in the distance—its slim, silver casing agleam, its chrome-orange warhead refracting a hot needle of light. The land's original courthouse rose beyond, a tall salmon-colored relic with dusted corner towers and pearl Renaissance gables. As the addict paced on, the stone Citadel loomed over the highway with its narrow dome stabbing up into the Midwestern sky.

It was the burglar's last crime that brought him near the old justice hall that afternoon. Two weeks before, he had prowled into an isolated farmhouse outside Ceresco. The place was classic Nebraska: wooden, flanked by lawns and maple trees, a chipped red barn, hickory-smoked sheds that almost touched the cornstalks. The property belonged to a ninety-four-year-old woman who had been moved to a nursing home.

The addict wasted no time in tearing through the elderly woman's world. He grabbed her curio cabinet, her stained glass door, her gramophone, her carnival glass wedding basket, her antique headboard, her antique doll rocker, her classic rocking chair. Before burning a cloud of dust up County Road A, he had also claimed her dresser, dishware, floor lamp, vases and even her butter churns.

The addict drove onto Highway 77 toward Lincoln. He knew he had looted far more antiques than he had managed to pilfer in his last break-in, which took place near Wahoo before Christmas. The bounty from that farmhouse intrusion was mostly clothes and furniture, though at one desperate point the addict had resorted to stripping the building of its triple-wall chimney pipe. But the elderly woman's treasury of collectibles was a major score—worth real cash in the city. If he could find a wealthy antiques collector who didn't ask many questions, it would be a windfall for bankrolling his methamphetamine habit. As it turns out, the collector who was pulled into the web soon phoned law enforcement, suspecting the items he had bought were connected to a burglary spree flashed across the local newspaper.

In February, a Saunders County sheriff's detective tracked the addict down. The investigator landed a confession to the burglaries and got the remaining antiques back from the addict's girlfriend and grandmother. The addict eventually took the officer who had arrested him on a driving tour of the raided farm properties.

Authorities assumed at least one series of crimes was over. They were wrong.

On the same March afternoon the addict was granted conditional release from jail, the forty-seven-year-old could not make it out of the courthouse bathroom without dropping his face on a line of methamphetamine. Two days later, a Saunders County sheriff's deputy caught him scampering across a roof as he burglarized yet another farmhouse.

SAUNDERS COUNTY is seven hundred square miles of corn sown with bean fields, grain elevators and a scatter shot of little towns. In late August light, the sun and evening wind play on the bodies of corn, until they go tipping like green stems ruffled in dry, crisp gold under a sea of rusty needles. It's the adagio of the former prairie; a dance of sorrel breeze bending that appears to shudder, almost imperceptively, on the edge of the faint, honey-glazed dusk.

An armada of John Deere tractors lines the gateway to Wahoo, which, save for three chain diners and a battery of empty storefronts, is nearly identical to how it looked in 1979, the year Hollywood tycoon Darryl Zanuck passed away. The man who gave American cinema "The Jazz Singer," "The King and I" and "The Grapes of Wrath" was raised amidst the lurching, open-geared gas tractors of Wahoo. Ten years into the new millenium, mornings are alive with elders floating in and out of C&C's Café, some talking about grandchildren, crops or world events, others reading Jack's Tillman's "Our Town" column in the local newspaper. School buses roll by Hackberry Park, where the baseball diamond is half surrounded by a primrose blanket of corn stocks. When night comes, bottles bat inside the 6th Street Garage as men gather for fantasy football drafts, televised NASCAR and rounds of pool. A farmer's world turns on the seasons; and the county's energy courses strong in autumn, when families pack a broad aluminum ziggurat to cheer the Wahoo Warriors, pushing them to spread some gridiron mayhem against whichever high school football team from eastern Nebraska has wandered into their domain.

One person who enjoys these frames of Saunders County is its sheriff, Kevin Stukenholtz. A former captain with the Nebraska State Troopers, Stukenholtz is proud to live in a stretch of farmland filled with "good schools, good churches and good people." He likes knowing his neighbors. He's happy to recognize nearly every face at a youth sporting event. With an office adjacent to the county museum, he thinks Saunders residents do an admirable job of honoring their history while finding ways to survive the bludgeoning economic truths that have gutted rural communities across the United States.

Yet, as the county's top cop, Stukenholtz also sees the disease lurking under all of the Americana—he knows what shadows fall over the silos.

When Stukenholtz learned in March of 2010 that a serial

burglar had posted bail, snorted meth in his courthouse and was apprehended forty-eight hours later for breaking into another farmhouse, the veteran cop wasn't shocked; vaguely curious about the suspect's level of compulsive desperation, but not shocked. In eastern Nebraska, commercial theft and residential burglary are instinctive survival mechanisms of those hooked on methamphetamine. Stukenholtz's deputies routinely encounter construction sites that have been stripped bare of copper and aluminum wire, or farming equipment that's been plundered for steel parts and radiators. "Basically, if someone's on meth, then metal theft is their primary occupation," is how Stukenholtz explains the situation to farmers and foremen. "These guys will be up for two or three days straight without sleep, finally crash; and then wake up to spend a whole afternoon stealing any object or implement they can recycle, just to get a hundred dollars to buy more meth."

In all of his days wearing a badge, Stukenholtz has yet to investigate even one metal theft in which dependency on the drug wasn't the underlying cause. But builders and farmers—two groups throughout Nebraska already stressed to the breaking point by the recession—aren't the only citizens targeted by the predatory eyes of the hyper-stimulated: Quaint generational farmhouses lost in the tall green-golden crops often fall victim to the hungers of the local meth world. According to Stukenholtz, too many senior citizens living in retirement facilities have experienced the shock of knowing their houses were dismantled by meth users, their belongings removed, their antiques snatched, their family heirlooms gone forever.

In June 2010, the man who inhaled a line of meth inside the Saunders County courthouse before engaging in his fourth residential break-in of the year, pleaded guilty to felony burglary and was sent to state prison for a decade. The knocking of the gavel meant there was one less fast-fingered drug dependent for Stukenholtz's deputies to hunt down. But there will always be another. For the deputies, the burglar's unremarkable name begins to fade. Long shifts and stacks of paperwork blunt its significance. Some officers will forget its five-prong syllable cadence altogether: because his name is incidental. All that matters is what the man represents to the blond, swaying stalks of the open countryside. In Saunders, his story is many stories. There, he is simply the addict.

Rural Cass County, which neighbors Saunders, has been engaged in the same ongoing struggle with methamphetamine. In 2008, this quiet stretch of land around the Platte River had twenty-three meth labs reported, structures with old oxblood sinks and noxious garages that kept the drug moving to the tidy streets of Louisville, or the creek-cradled hamlet of Weeping Water. And the bathtub dust blowing through Cass also spreads over the state line to Mills County, Iowa, where the sharp, shallow peaks of the Loess hills bump a ruptured spine through wooded landfalls and wet ranges of holly-colored soy. Blanketing elm and maple trees cover streams that flow down the high terrain to cities like Glenwood. Every August, children from across Mills County come to Glenwood to jump onto small, foot-pedaled John Deere replicas for the annual youth tractor pull. The spectacle of little overalls and mad wheeling belongs to Keg Creek Days, an annual showcase of the city's pride in its legacy of Missouri River-dwellers, from Paleo-Indians to German and Swedish pioneers. September Homecoming is a bigger event that's dominated by sixty-year class reunions riding floats in the parade while families stroll by opulent brick churches and Italianate homes, or 1st Street's turn-of-the-century movie theater.

Mills County has fifteen thousand residents. Its entire population fits into a quarter of Kinnick Stadium at the University of Iowa. Fifteen thousand residents—and thirty-four churches. But, in 2010, the question of whether the laboratory scourge of the farmlands has touched this community is answered by simply clicking on the sheriff's official webpage. Operated out of an old brick office that county lawmen have been using since before Prohibition, the webpage is clean, simple, decidedly modest. Two-thirds of its content falls under the heading, "What is methamphetamine?" The text below is broken into topics like, "What are methamphetamines?" "What do they look like?" "What are the physical side effects?" "What are the psychological effects and risks?" "Why do young people become users and abusers?"

In the weeks leading up to the 2010 Keg Creek Days celebration, Mills County residents reported numerous thefts and burglaries to law enforcement; and two suspected methamphetamine traffickers were arrested in neighboring Montgomery County, an even more rural sliver of Iowa.

Methamphetamine made its way from California to the Midwest in the late 1980s. As it began landing in small towns from Kansas to Indiana, so did Lance Morrison.

Today the boys in blue just call him "Cap," but in the decades that methamphetamine was growing from a rash of crime tremors along California's coast to a full fault line of tragedy, Lance Morrison was probing for scientific responses. Highly philosophical, deadly observant, often sympathetic, Morrison was the Newark Police Department's unofficial Rhodes scholar. His work with the Southern Alameda County Narcotics Enforcement Team became a depressing seismograph of meth's arrival in the Golden State's bay; and Morrison guessed before many it was the coming of a mainshock epidemic.

Morrison began to read all of the medical data he could find about amphetamines. He learned the ways they leech on the biochemistry of the human brain. He memorized their psychomotor effects and suppressant abilities. His insights accelerated as he began videotaping interviews with meth addicts he'd put in handcuffs, eventually becoming an expert at catching the symptoms: Blitzkrieg pulse, dribbling pupils, chewing cigarettes with the front of the teeth, sweat coming through the face instead of down it. He also began to understand the different species of addicts he was encountering: There was the rail-snorter, content to drive his or her neurostimulants out of the skull in a slow blizzard of dust. There was the needle hound, who hit meth with cold metal, pushing it through the epidermis, slipping its venom on a red, fluid freeway to the brain. And then there were those who bowed to crystal meth, finding the ultimate way to bypass the liver, that a holy smoke-router into the lungs and straight to the central nervous system. No breakdown in the organs. No travel time in the hemoglobin. Just pure gaseous daggers of methamphetamine hitting the brain all at once.

The more Cap talked to users in custody, the more he realized that the various species of addicts were subject to the same terminus point—that their stories ended in the same neurological abyss. When a person first takes methamphetamine, feelings of satisfaction, elevation, invincibility course into the body. Hunger doesn't come. Sleep doesn't come. Spoken lies can become real. Manipulation equals control. Every thought equals supremacy. But a change comes over the brain with that imprint of the first meth experience, and the cerebrum's delicate reward and motivational systems are utterly murdered by the pursuit of experiencing the first high again. Morrison saw the path. A user becomes an addict when the rush begins to end faster, leaving a ravaged head that chases a memory of first contact, often at the cost of children, work, families and friends. The addict goes on runs and crashes. When the grip releases, the addict feels low, paranoid, emotionally abandoned. Methamphetamine is all that the addict begins thinks about, pounding more and more into the body just to feel normal, just to go to work, just to get out of bed. For every meth user Morrison arrested who fit the stereotype of being hyper-twitched, he found just as many who admitted they felt horrible—that they were confused, sleep-deprived, jittery and depressed. Morrison began telling his fellow police officers, "We keep thinking about meth addicts as people who are always high; but I tend to think of most of them as individuals who can't get high at all."

Such observations had Morrison traveling across the country. The proliferation of methamphetamine into the Midwestern United States pushed unsuspecting law enforcement back on their heels. By the early 1990s, Nebraska cops like Stukenholtz were being warned by California police officers, "Once meth hits your cities, you'll wish you had cocaine and heroin back." Word began to spread that a West Coast narcotics officer out of Newark had compiled a video montage of meth addicts that was like nothing law enforcement outside of California had ever seen. Morrison started teaching seminars on methamphetamine to cops in Nebraska, Iowa, Kansas and Indiana. He felt good about the strengthening dialog; but on October 18, 1995, Cap himself would come face-to-face with the ultimate meaning of meth-driven violence.

The incident began when 32-year-old Stephen Vanderveer—the son of a prominent newspaper personality—was gorging himself on meth inside a home on Milani Avenue in Newark. He was smoking the drug with a longtime female friend, Norene Kovach. At the time, Vanderveer and Kovach were both under federal indictment for selling meth linked to a million-dollar laboratory in the California's central Delta, allegedly run by the Hells Angels. They were out on bail that night when, around 11:15 p.m., the nucleus accumbens in Vanderveer's skull began literally cooking. He raised a loaded gun, peered over at Kovach and leveled the barrel directly in her face. He squeezed the trigger four times to see what would happen. Next, he calmly picked up a telephone, telling the 911 dispatcher, "I just shot someone. Don't bother sending an ambulance, just send the police."

Morrison was the first unit to respond. The sergeant was alone when he pulled up to the victim's ranch-style house. Veering quickly into the driveway, he broke out of his cruiser and moved by Kovach's 1988 silver Jaguar. Vanderveer swept onto the deck. For an instant his hands were empty; but, as Morrison shouted orders, he reached behind his back and drew a pistol with an extended silencer. "You're gonna have to kill me," he called out to the officer he had summoned. A few seconds. A cop's eternity. Morrison steadied his 9mm, yelling. The unhinged killer aimed his gun as he charged onto the lawn. Morrison opened fire.

Within minutes, Newark police officers moved beyond Vanderveer's body, probing the house to discover a dead woman whose facial features had been ruined by gunshot after gunshot.

Morrison kept teaching narcotics classes, kept traveling the U.S. and kept watching the meth world evolve. He would eventually become one of the most astute witnesses to methamphetamine's long, twisted and paradoxical history. The stimulant's abuse began in California in the early 1960s with Desoxyn and Methedrine, both legal, prescribed forms of methamphetamine. By the time pharmaceutical companies realized what they had unleashed, the first manifestation of the bathtub chemist had already arrived. He came in the form of the "prope-dope" cooker—a pawn of the Hells Angels' bid to control easy money flowing through the Bay Area's counter-culture. "Prope-dope," or phenyl-2-propanone derived meth, was a volatile chemical amalgam relying on toxic sparks like ammonia, mercury and hydrochloric acid. "It came out different colors," bikers would later remember. "It smelled like cat piss."

Soon, outlaw motorcycle gangs up and down the West Coast were working with "prope-dope" cookers to supply a new population of meth addicts. The federal Drug Enforcement Agency struck back in 1980, changing the law to make propanone impossible to get. Overnight, the Red-P cookers replaced the prope-dope masters on the food chain, offering the Meth World a quicker, more addictive recipe for its engine. Their tool kit of ephedrine, iodine and matchbook strikers was easier to get, easier to handle and easier to hide. The "Nazi method" was also on the rise, cooking meth with pseudoephedrine, anhydrous ammonia, lye, paint thinner and lithium extracted from batteries.

Methamphetamine production in California was booming. So were meth exports to Oregon, Washington and the farming communities of the Midwest. By the mid-1990s, California's Attorney General Dan Lungren was being told by his bureau chiefs that, if each state in the U.S. was its own country, then California would be the country supplying all the other countries with their methamphetamine.

In 2005, the U.S. Department of Justice believed it could knock down the plague by targeting the availability of ephedrine. Motorcycle gangs and white cookers countered the move by reaching out to Mexican nationals. From Jalisco to Durango, drug cartels could obtain and control large supplies of ephedrine, propanone and virtually any chemical precursor the United States attempted to block from its public. For outlaw bikers, a move for survival spelled the end of supremacy over the Meth World. Mexican-operated clandestine labs began appearing up and down the Highway 99 corridor in southern and central California. Backed by well-meaning U.S. policy, the cartels managed to take over the lion's share of the meth trade in the western United States.

Morrison watched it all happen — a worming metamorphosis through wretched bodies and the wreckage of lives.

The 2005 ephedrine crackdown hasn't broken meth's stranglehold on rural Nebraska and Iowa, though it has greatly reduced clandestine laboratories. When Stukenholtz first began working in Saunders County in 2004, his department's specially equipped van for cleaning meth labs was, in his words, "rolling almost every week." The sheriff's brother, a cop who works in neighboring Sharpe County, was finding even more makeshift laboratories, at times raiding two or three different cooking operations in one night, all housed within the same country motel.

For the moment, reports of clandestine laboratories in Iowa

and Nebraska are down more than 70 percent, according to the Office of National Drug Control Policy. But, as the police chief of Cass County's largest city told the *Plattsmouth Journal* in 2009, "The pseudo ephedrine law has been successful in reducing the labs, but not the use." And Mexican drug traffickers have taken full advantage of this cultural cancer, moving powder and crystal from California across the Midwest on Interstate 80, crossing Nebraska and Iowa, all the way to Indiana. Nebraska law enforcement agencies have a common saying about these "dope cars," declaring, "If they're heading east, they're full of meth; if they're heading west, they're full of money."

The market for methamphetamine in the Midwest remains. The physical and cultural hunger remains. People often ask Stukenholtz if it's the economy, the hard times and the financial hopelessness of America's heartland that are behind the crimes they read about in the newspaper. The sheriff's answer never waivers: "Throughout my entire law enforcement career, I've never seen an honest, hard-working person lose their job and then turn to stealing from others," Stukenholtz tells them. "No matter how desperate, those blue-collar folks seem to always find a way to take care of themselves. They cut back on things. They let things go. They do other work if they have to. But they stay honest. No, it's the meth addicts who are stealing from their neighbors. It's what they do. To them, stealing is basically a full-time job."

CHAPTER 3

Jackson, California: May 21

CHRIS RICE'S PATROL car stalks down Broadway Avenue, a lined clutter of immaculately restored Victorian houses with trimmed lawns on the north side, and paint-splintered hovels, broken toys and overgrown weeds along the south. At 6-foot-2, 215 pounds, Rice is hardly a cop who invites physical confrontation. Broad shouldered, with a red beard and clean-shaven head, he's already arrested six hundred individuals in a city of fewer than six thousand. Not too many have had the instinct—or inanity—to test his resolve. But Rice knows that Christopher Jarod Stockton might go the other way. The parolee-at-large is 6-foot-4 and 255 pounds. The last time he exited prison, most of that weight was pure muscle. Rice can spot Stockton in an instant: The predatory eyes, the Samson-shaped jaw, the creed "nothing's sacred" in a woven tattoo across the shelf of his pecs.

A year ago, one of Rice's partners, a blunt-talking, Irish-blooded veteran named Mike Collins, got the drop on Stockton at gunpoint. It started under an overhang on South Avenue when Collins and another JPD uniform rolled up to hit the door with a warrant. The girl they were checking on peered through a crack. "Where's your baby?" Collins asked. The baby was with the grandparents, she answered. Collins and his backup immediately moved in to search the house, gliding past louvered blinds and a pipe clouded with charred crystal meth in plain view on the coffee table. Collins found a familiar addict upstairs who warned him that someone else was in the house. As the cop slipped down into the garage, thirty-one years of working every crime beat known to the badge drew his eyes to an "L" cove closet under the stairs. His hand slowly reached for the doorknob. In an instant, Stockton was looking directly into the barrel of Collins' .40 caliber.

That was spring of 2009. Now it's spring 2010 and Stockton is the talk around a dull-colored coffeemaker in Rice's police station. He's out of jail again. He's violated parole again. He's back in Jackson again. The guys have to bring him in again.

Rice wouldn't mind being the one.

Two men could not be more different than Christopher Stockton and Christopher Rice. Rice grew up in the California foothills. His love for hick expressions, souped-up cars and twang-laden music earned him the moniker "Country Bumpkin" in the police academy. After a while, the cadets just started calling him "Bumpkin." When Amador County began pushing for specialized narcotics detectives in 2007, primarily to battle crime around methamphetamine, Rice was tapped to be the Jackson Police Department's go-to man. He's since earned a reputation with cops and suspects alike as a tough, thorough narcotics agent. The only thing that angers him as much as chemical cookers and absentee meth moms are excuses for lazy police work.

Stockton, on the other hand, came out of the California

Central Valley, a registered narcotics offender with a rap sheet in three counties. He's spent time behind bars for residential burglary, grand theft, selling methamphetamine and vandalism. Jackson cops have noticed that his name appears in other investigations even when he's not the lead suspect. It's not clear what first brought Stockton to the Gold Country. What is known is that he was collared in a meth house on South Avenue—a house that usually has a baby in it.

The cruiser inches along Broadway's south sidewalk with its light bar passing under the knotted limbs of cigar trees. A mailbox painted like the American flag sits ajar. A half-open yard gate stoops down on its hinges. Rice comes to the house where informants claim Stockton is hiding, a non-descript address that's one street away from where Collins pulled his gun on the Giant.

Slowing near the driveway, Rice catches the flash of a swinging door. He sees the streak of a flattop, a naked shoulder blurring between the wall and a van, and then a large torso clambering around pollen-powdered garbage lids. Rice hits the accelerator. His seat belt breaks open. The patrol car swings into a U-turn on the soundless avenue, fast, fluid, deliberate. Its tires lock in without even a skid. The massive form of a man swings around. Rice's hand is on the door when he sees that the head staring back at him belongs to a stout figure draped in a toga-sized jersey. The man is holding an infant in a loose diaper. He's not Stockton.

The patrol car begins to crawl. "He has to come out eventually," Rice tells himself as he drives down to the parking lot of an abandoned grocery store on the edge of the city. Stopping, he gets out to make sure that a group of transients hasn't broken in again, converting the thirty-six-thousand square-foot structure into a petty theft emporium. The faces that could morph through the glass are frequent flyers with cops in the area—drunks, probationers, parolees and meth addicts who have hit the lowest ebb, the ranks of the rural homeless, living on handouts and burglary. While most hardened "tweeks" reside in sheltered squalor rather than the America's open countrysides, Jackson has dealt with a band of homeless addicts roving from empty dwellings on its outskirts, to hidden camps under its bridges, buildings and even its library.

Seeing that the doors to the empty structure haven't been tampered with, Rice crosses the highway to check the permanent transient camp just minutes away, fortified under the dim sanctuary of a highway underpass. Some of Rice's fellow officers try to avoid the cavern without backup under the hard-won knowledge that transient addicts are impossible to predict. A few weeks ago, a cop working ten miles west in the city of Ione had a strange encounter with a homeless meth-worshiper named Justen Solansky. It was in the hottest part of the afternoon. Solanksy was dancing wildly in the street when the Ione police car approached him. Moments before, the young addict had been wrapped in a blanket as he stood on the top of a pickup truck and spoke a blathered soliloquy to the sky. Now, he was gyrating in the roadway, baked in sweat, naked to the waist with his zipper down—a fevered human knot of rhythmic convulsions. His limbs were swinging, his legs fighting against the rigid, black leather threads. It was a textbook Ice flight: claims of visions, paranoid agitation, constant tick-turning movements. "You're going to have to take me to jail!" Solansky blurted to the officer. He reached down into the perspiration pools welling in his trousers and ripped out two crystal meth pipes. "See! See!"

The story made Rice shake his head.

With the day brightening, Rice hops the guardrails and chicken-wire fence the state of California has erected, due to complaints, to keep transients out of the concrete corridor. He makes his way down a steep embankment to the mouth of the cave. His flashlight moves, slowly probing, cutting an eye over beds embedded in the loose dirt, a stream of empty beer cans, scattered piles of garbage and torn sleeping rolls covered in mounds of bat feces. He's sure there won't be any methamphetamine left here. It's too valuable to them. Emerging on the other side in the sunlight, he reaches into a rusty pipe lodged in the blackberry vines. His arm goes in, pulling out five wasted, unmatched sneakers. Experience has taught the detective that if addicts have something to hide, they usually resort to thrown-out shoes. Carefully tugging on his gloves, Rice maneuvers his fingers inside: No used baggies with residue, though he does get a full bottle of prescription muscle relaxers, which he knows were being downed with cheap beer from cans littered around the camp site.

Twenty years ago, the idea of Jackson, California, having a transient population was unthinkable. But that was before the city met hard times. In 1997, its only semblance of industry—a rusty lumber mill employing hundreds of men—closed down for good. Some Jacksonians felt the one hope for survival would be a tourism boom from the city's ambiance as a Gold Rush destination. It was a dream predicated on the Main Street microcosm: a hope for breathing life into the historic avenue by filling it with novelties, antique shops and charming merchants from bygone eras. Ultimately, livelihood would depend on visitors drinking from an illusion of California's past, thrusting their imaginations into what Jackson looks like in postcards, the gold-capped crucifix of Saint Patrick's Church lifting against the clouds, or its twin steeple rising from the Methodist church like some vague collision between a German town square and the American prairie, or the burnt ocher spine of the Argonaut head frame, a rotting memorial to the worst gold mining disaster in U.S. history; and, of course, Saint Sava's church, the oldest Serbian Orthodox icon in all of North America—that ghost on rainy afternoons fixed over the silent cemeteries.

For a while tourists came. The business owners eked by, employing as many people as they could manage. They tried hard to continue the traditions of sponsoring youth athletics, donating to the Interfaith Food Bank and arranging special benefits for families who were struggling with everything from spinal cord injuries to children with cancer. But the plan was threatened in 2008, when the shockwaves from Wall Street's turmoil had a far-reaching effect throughout the California Mother Lode. Tourism fell off a cliff. Television news stations began airing stories about Jackson's travails that featured images of taped-up windows and "For Rent" signs hanging above doors. Distant politicians began chanting modifications about "helping Wall Street to save Main Street." People in Jackson looked empty. As financial earthquakes continued to rumble through the U.S. economy, Jackson became part of the tragedy of Main Street America, a symbol for small business owners plummeting into financial crisis. By October of 2008, there were eighteen empty storefronts down Jackson's venerated corridor. The local newspaper printed a headline that read "Exodus on Main Street."

Now, on some winter dawns, campfire smoke rises from the

underpass, the most salient trace of an otherwise invisible problem in the city. But not invisible to Collins, who has ambled through Jackson's cemetery in the new light, his breath slowly steaming in pearl-flickered vapors as he looked at men hunched on slabs or curled under old, icy headstones. He's even discovered a few of the homeless slumbering beyond the doors of family crypts they've pushed their way into. The problem is also not invisible to Rice, who's spent afternoons stepping over obliterated glass in condemned addresses turned into flophouses, tiles covered in shredded mattresses, heaped layers of food, a menagerie of tipped bottles bleeding cinnamon amebas on the floor.

The detective climbs back over the wire fence to get in his patrol car. He takes another look up Broadway Avenue, scanning for Stockton. The street is dim. Lifeless. His Impala crosses the highway to the office of a nonprofit group that runs Jackson's safety house for battered women, where, waiting for him, is the shelter's director, Tammie Crabtree.

Ask a Jackson cop to summarize the director's job duties and you'll likely hear that Tammie Crabtree waits alone in dark parking lots until one in the morning, trying to find hotel rooms for abused mothers who call her phone all night, begging for help, and then don't show up to meet her. An officer might also point out that Tammie Crabtree spends tired Monday mornings explaining to women that she installed cameras around the shelter to stop addicts from sneaking methamphetamine inside, while seconds later assuring them that it's still a safe place to find refuge. A colleague would likely add that Tammie Crabtree—short, young and attractive—stands toe-to-toe with "cranked-out" wife beaters who storm into her office, demanding to have access to their victims. Any Jackson cop would certainly mention that Tammie Crabtree goes home every night anticipating a call from her husband, Josh, a sheriff's detective who works in the epicenter of the meth problem in Calaveras, the next rural county south. A friend like Rice even knows that Tammie Crabtree has watched skeletal female addicts get brought to the driveway of her personal residence, crater-cut and confused, mumbling in front of her children.

"And how's the most stubbornly hopeful person I know?" Rice asks as he tromps in with his thumbs tucked into his belt.

There's a shrug and smile. "Still hopeful," she replies. "Most of the time."

But even the indomitable Tammie Crabtree doesn't always understand the truth in that statement. Methamphetamine use is an ever-haunting demon inside the women's shelter. Its own surveys indicate that one-third of the women checking in have fled a dangerous confrontation in which either the victim, abuser, or both, are under the influence of illegal drugs. Methamphetamine is the most consistent trigger pin. And Crabtree is honest that the number of victims coming to her from meth houses is far higher than what the documentation shows. The truth only flashes from the sides of a bleak carousel: Women coming and going, flushed, bruised jaws like somatic skin puzzles, break-ups and reconciliations, the deadly cocktail of addiction, pain and control, all of these have made Tammie Crabtree an expert on the devastation of meth-inspired violence.

Rice and Crabtree talk briefly about a new case that's come up. Before Rice exits out of the doorway, he says, "You always try to keep us upbeat, Tammie."

Smiling, she throws back, "God knows we need to be."

Rice gives a weary nod. Still, it's hard for him: He's seen too much since being a narcotics officer—especially when it comes to small, worried eyes glancing upward. He thinks about a local meth mom whom one of his fellow officers still refers to as "I'll Never Forget Clare." It was February of 2005 when Jackson cops launched a welfare check on Clare's apartment, worried about her children. Clare opened the door fumbling a naked two-year-old in her arms. Before the policemen could move, she'd knocked the baby's head against a wall with her quick, tripping body ticks. Within seconds the officers knew what they had. Clare flashed the mannerisms of a spasmic swan. Her pupils were half-screwed. Her pulse was racing. She was ordered to sit down as the cops made their way toward two other children beyond a wasteland of spoiled food and garbage. Pausing, one officer yanked open a dresser to see a cloud of flies boiling off the dark, rotted fruit Clare had tucked under her shirts. Another officer entered the kitchen and immediately froze: Amidst crusted dishes and piles of trash, he saw a large bowl full of human urine on the kitchen counter. He soon found another bowl full of urine hidden inside the pantry, where the family's food was kept. By this time, his partner was moving into what months before had been a new apartment bathroom. Now the space was desecrated by a toilet overflowing with bodily waste. A tiny training toilet to the left of it was just as ruined. The officer almost vomited when he realized that the bathroom contained several neatly tied plastic bags stuffed full of human excrement.

A Rosetta Stone for the smeared filth was waiting on the kitchen table—a plate loaded with white powder next to a baggie of methamphetamine. The officers pieced together that Clare had been "cutting the dope" with her Albertson's club card before snorting it up a straw. The mother was placed in handcuffs. Her children were soon led away from the apartment by child protective services. Three months later, "I'll Never Forget Clare" pleaded guilty to felony child abuse and possession of methamphetamine.

It's only one case; but Rice can think of dozens. He can remember searching the apartment of a young woman named Amber in November of 2008, finding three small children alone in dimensions of food refuse, near a bathtub filled with grimy brown swill. Rice and the other investigators were soon looking at their reports, trying to find tactful ways to describe the pornographic photos of Amber they'd discovered amidst the crystal meth pipes, digital scales and baggies of methamphetamine they were taking into evidence. One officer would make sure to mention a stack of explicit nude pictures of the mother that had been left within reach of her children. Amber pleaded guilty to several charges. Her sentence was suspended on the condition of treatment for meth addiction.

And what did the 2008 treatment stint do for Amber? Two months ago, Rice was the Jackson detective who charged her with sneaking methamphetamine into jail, after she'd been caught by a sheriff's deputy transporting the drug through one of the county beats.

Rice turns down Main Street.

He can hear the names echo: Amber, "I'll Never Forget Clare" and, of course, Matthew David. It was the morning of October 22, 2009, when Amador County probation agents swept a house on the south side of Broadway Avenue. Red flags went up, and the agents soon called for Jackson police and a narcotics investigator. That was the day Rice began hunting Matthew again.

It was the tall, slim form of Officer Mike Collins speaking with Matthew's girlfriend that greeted Rice when he drove onto the scene. Matthew David was a known fugitive. Surrounded by the ever-growing constellation of badges, the girl gave him up, admitting that her man was hiding downstairs with the couple's two-year-old daughter. The announcement that she'd left Matthew alone with the baby that morning caused a probation agent to make a beeline for the stairway. Matthew, a chronic meth user, had already been convicted of felony child abuse and other serious crimes. The agent hurried through a shut bedroom door to find the little toddler screaming "Daddy!" near an open window. The child was holding a crystal meth pipe at her mouth and standing by two bags of methamphetamine.

Matthew David's flight from the room on Broadway was short-lived. Rice testified against him in January of 2010, telling a judge not only about the recovered drugs, but exactly how they had found the baby. Before Matthew's trial began, he pleaded guilty to felony child endangerment and was sentenced to four years in state prison. A judge offered the convicted man a word of advice on his way out the door: Give up methamphetamine, or spend the rest of his life continuing to "swirl the toilet bowl."

Rice makes another pass up Broadway Avenue, driving by the house where Matthew David abandoned his two-year-old daughter to chance. It's one block away from the south city address where Christopher Stockton is hiding. This is the new criminal history of Jackson, California; worlds apart from the events that once made the place infamous. At the dawn of the 1950s, Jackson's main street was lined with a fleet of shining Chryslers and Chevrolets. Overhead, a clutter of marquees jutted from grocery stores, druggists, banks, theaters and eighteen freewheeling saloons. There were dice tumbling inside the Pioneer Rex. There was blackjack and roulette beyond the batting doors of the Louvre Club. There were also five houses of ill repute open for business in broad daylight. Jackson was known as Little Reno, the little city that could—declare the state and all its laws subservient to the will of third-generation loggers, ranchers and miners. Right or wrong, good or bad, it remains California's strangest example of rural self-determinism.

Today, the tale of The Great Jackson Vice Probe reads like a flickering neon legend: In 1955, the city's mayor, councilmen and police department were all indicted for keeping the town "wide open" for gambling and prostitution. The years leading up to this court spectacle saw a massive boom in tourism. Tunnels were dug. Secret doorways were cut into brick ramparts. Busses filled with college boys from Stockton and Sacramento rolled down Main Street every weekend. Cash was flowing through a small network of bank accounts.

California's Attorney General Pat Brown began threatening the city fathers through speeches to newspapers. He was coolly ignored. As Brown's scrutiny increased, the oldest, strictest English teacher at Jackson High School came out publicly in favor of prostitution, announcing that the brothels preserved the reputation of her girls by keeping troublesome boys distracted. Brown issued new ultimatums, but the pocket-lining insurrection continued.

And then—a reckoning. In 1953, the Jackson City Council accidently hired an honest police chief: His name was George Milardovich and he was a tough-as-nails U.S. Marine who had fought in the worst moments of Pearl Harbor, Guadalcanal,

Guam and Iwo Jima. Milardovich soon made it clear that he viewed the city council as "morally corrupt." He had even less respect for its five portly members because they hadn't served in the war. Bent on restoring the integrity of the police, the Marine drew an unmistakable line in the sand. It was obvious he was tampering with fortunes. City fathers tried intimidation. Their obstacle wouldn't budge. Anonymous death threats started coming in. But Milardovich couldn't be bought off nor frightened away. A near-deadly stare down ensued as the attorney general's agents swept in to back the solitary police chief. And then, with the trumpets of the new century sounding, the walls came tumbling down.

It's this colorful legacy of the 1950s, as much as the shadows of the Gold Rush, that the merchants of Main Street hang onto. For them, Jackson is the rebellious side of the western dream. It's a place where the wildest freedom — no matter how corrupt — was clung to beyond its sunset. It's a place where the last great confederacy of good old boys got rich off the illusion of progress. And it's a place where a single lawman took a stand, according to his code, and never backed down. Jackson is the West, and the end of the West. It's a monument to the final gasping breath of an American vision.

As Rice's patrol car turns off Broadway, it slides past the doorstep of George Milardovich, who, at ninety-two-years-old, has lived to see that vision end. The Marine who fired his rifle at Japanese planes soaring over Pearl Harbor, who battled Imperial soldiers on the cliffs of Iwo Jima, who brought down a ring of bar-side casinos and pleasure palaces and made it respectable for men like Rice and Collins to wear a Jackson police uniform again, still lives on Bright Avenue. It's one street away from the city's homeless shelter, from the house where parolee-at-large Christopher Stockton is hiding and from the window that Matthew David jumped out of, leaving his baby alone with a crystal meth pipe clasped in her tiny hands.

CHAPTER 4
Falling Under a Big Sky

CLAD IN A COTTON T-shirt, a fleck of white paint on his left cheek, Leonard Dunning shifted his eyes down as a jailer snapped his mug shot. For an instant, the gravity of it all looked to resonate through the strong, chiseled lines of his face. Living in a Montana county that averages three people per square mile, Dunning could likely hear his legacy playing out in the ranches, bars and cafes that dot the broken plains of Custer territory. Who was he? Leonard Forest Dunning: father, businessman, community volunteer, 20-year rescue worker, Captain of the Miles City Fire Department—and accused meth dealer.

On August 27, 2009, Dunning was brought into a courtroom in Miles City and arraigned on two counts of criminal possession of methamphetamine with intent to distribute by accountability, both felonies; one charge of use or possession of property subject to criminal forfeiture, a felony; and one charge of possession of drug paraphernalia. The judge made it very clear to Dunning—who had spent the better part of his adult life trying to save the lives of others—that, if convicted, he was facing substantial time in state prison.

A REARING CRY, hoofs clanking steel, and then the banging swing of a gate's rusted jaw. The horse's hindquarters are 6-feet skyward as a dust ghost twines under them. The rider holds his rope, knuckling down on a mean advance of fear-fueled lunges. His Windrider hat tucks south. His free hand reaches for the air. A bleary string of cowboys quivers by, their salt-burned forms clinging to the chewed, white top of the chute line. Below, a neck of pure muscle hardens like a stump. The rider throws all his torque against it, until the matted cluster of fur and tendons goes toppling ahead, hooves stabbed inward to rake the exploding dirt. It's jarring. The bronc's eyes are black, nostrils flared. The animal's back legs land down, his muzzle drops and his shoulders go hitching high for the faded planks of the announcer's booth: Its mane shudders in a cracked blur, a whip melted intrinsically into the blasted fringe of the rider's chaps. The young man survives the burst; but his opponent is charging up now. Soil-socking kicks. Vicious little prances. Three colossal jumps and a wicked half-turn launch the rider left, knees pitched over its spine, cowboy hat gone, blue cotton shirt like a canvas sail. All bones and impact.

Crawling in a red cloud, the rider can sense the horse gallop to the other side of the arena. The young man brushes his chaps and limps back to the gate on a pair of unsteady ankles. And the crowd exalts, clapping and whistling as his worn-out boot heels drag through the fuming, shattered earth.

The annual bucking horse sale is the premier event of Miles City, a place that southeastern Montanans still consider "one of the last genuine cowboy towns on the western frontier." On the third weekend of every May, thousands of rodeo fanatics pour into the city, the seat of Custer County, located at the

Yellowstone and Tongue rivers some forty rugged miles south of the Terry Badlands. They come set on watching unbroken horses get ridden in a way that tips the cutter dents of their hats to history; because it was in this valley, just beyond the eroded puce hilltops of welded shale, that the Montana Stockgrowers' Association was formed in 1884. The Bucking Horse Sale is a symbol of those first grizzled range riders—a bridge to the hard-fought ranching heritage of the land. The people of Custer County know that it's not just giant shoulders they stand on, but damn tough ones, too.

In the weeks leading up to the 2009 Bucking Horse Sale, agents from the Eastern Montana Drug Task Force were eight minutes away from the rodeo arena surveying a house on Butler Street. Dan Baker was assigned to the force out of the Miles City Police Department and had been studying the Butler Street address since the beginning of the year. Neighbors were claiming pungent fumes emanated from the house. Even more concerning, a host of unknown vehicles were pulling in and out of its driveway at all hours of the night. In February, a confidential source informed agents that the house was indeed a sales point for methamphetamine. A special investigator from Yellowstone County named Ken Tuss agreed, informing the task force in April that a suspected meth dealer had been observed making trips from Billings, Montana to Miles City, straight to the house on Butler Street. The man in question was Keith Arnold.

As cowboys from across the high west were descending on Miles City for the World Famous Bucking Horse Sale, the pieces were all fitting together for Baker and the other task force agents. Arnold was living at the address. Cars were coming and going. The tips and intelligence seemed to keep checking out.

The only problem was the house belonged to Arnold's long-time friend, confidant and roommate, Leonard Dunning, a captain in the Miles City Fire Department; and it appeared Dunning was aware and involved in the meth activity.

On a warm night near the end of July, the dusk on Main Street was cut by slim rods of neon carnation, the piercing lights of the Montana Bar, the Indian-red glow of a creature strutting on the Bison Bar's marquee. Ranch trucks pushed their head-lights down the tan brickwork of the avenue, passing the 600 Club, the First Presbyterian Church and the Kickin' Ass Hat Company. As night gave way to dark morning hours, a single pickup truck crept with its lights off down the alley behind Dunning's house. Agent Baker was behind the wheel. Two members of the task force were at his side. The truck slowed near a trash rack on the northeast corner of Dunning's property. Slipping out, the agents lifted two large garbage bags up from the rack and dropped them into the back of the truck. Within seconds the corner was empty again.

For Baker, the trash collection amounted to polypropylene-wrapped Christmas presents: a broken digital scale, crystal meth pipes and a light bulb turned into a meth burner. It was all the agents needed to get a search warrant on Dunning's house.

On August 25, news that a Miles City fire captain and his roommate had been arrested for distributing meth spread through southeastern Montana like a herd of spooked antelope. *The Miles City Star, The Billings Gazette* and *The Missoulian* all carried the story. Most television newscasts throughout Montana pushed shorter versions across the airwaves and on their websites. The following Thursday, Dunning was arraigned in the Custer County Courthouse. He stood as Judge Gary Day told him that the maximum penalty was twenty-five years in state prison. Dunning pleaded not guilty to all charges.

IN THE WAKE OF Dunning's arrest, the fire department was open and cooperative with Miles City Star Editor, Marla Prell. Fire Chief Derrick Rodgers assured his hometown newspaper that Dunning had been immediately suspended, pending a full investigation by the city into his activities and the question of whether he had put the public at risk. Though hoping the newspaper wouldn't over-emphasize Dunning's role as fire captain, Rodgers also confirmed that a wider personnel sweep was under way to determine if methamphetamine use had crept into the culture of the Miles City Fire Department. The other firefighters would ultimately be cleared; but a seed of doubt had been planted for anyone in the public choosing to dwell on it, and it was doubt that was cast over those who were among Custer County's most visible community role models.

Some Montanans viewed Dunning's arrest as an indictment of Miles City itself, claiming it was proof that the cowboy capital of the West was actually a well-known "meth town," an image that had been growing since November of 2000, when 18-year-old Cassie Haydal was found dying on her bathroom floor from a meth-induced heart attack. Haydal was a bright, church-going honors student who volunteered for after-school programs and coached her sister's basketball team. She was part of a prominent Miles City family. She had countless friends: The revelation that Cassie had been using methamphetamine for more than a year shook Miles City to its core. Dozens of news stories followed about meth-related arrests in Miles City, culminating in a 2008 interview with Jeff Faycosh—a Miles City drug agent with the same task force that arrested Dunning—in which Fay-cosh observed that between 2002 and 2008, his officers seized 2,515 grams of methamphetamine and closed down 36 meth labs in the area. Throughout that time, Cassie Haydal's mother, the Miles City Star news staff and community leaders fought an ongoing battle to educate the public about meth addiction. From teachers to law enforcement, a sense of real progress was gradually building. Now, the statewide media blitz around Leonard Dunning's arrest once again linked Miles City to the stereotype of a meth-ridden drug den.

Dunning walked into city hall on September 15 and offered his official resignation from the fire department. Two days later, the former captain's attorney, Terry Hanson, appeared at the courthouse for Dunning's omnibus hearing. Hanson pored over the evidence presented by the task force. There were bags of methamphetamine found in Dunning's basement during the warrant search, along with one quarter-pound of marijuana. Any hopes that alleged drug dealer Keith Arnold was solely responsible for the crime appeared to evaporate when agents came across crystal meth pipes in Dunning's computer room and baggies containing a white powder residue in one of Dunning's firefighter uniforms. Agents also seized nearly $2,500 in cash hidden under a couch. Most observers thought Hanson's client was in for a long battle.

In the weeks following the omnibus hearing, the open terrain outside the courthouse grew spotted with sulphur-colored touches of fall. Miles City is shouldered against the south bank of the Yellowstone River. In autumn, black cottonwoods across its current turn radiant yellow, matching dry, goldenrod flames of wildflowers breaking along the sandbars. The trees fan under a wash of low hills scrubbed like blistered mounds of ash—hard, knuckled ridgelines that buck against the wide open blue, or the bone-white brushstrokes in the sky.

Horse owners in the city took advantage of the waning sunshine, bundled in flannels and denim vests as they trotted steeds around, cowboy hats and sunglasses set against the tumbling blond hues. Droves of outdoorsmen were pulling into Miles City. Their rangy, mud-splattered trucks filled the parking lots of every cheap motel along Haynes Avenue. At night the hunters could be glimpsed from Highway 12, cutting and sawing at flesh in the cold star-swept breeze, hanging gutted carcasses on frames under spotlights from buzzing generators, leaving hoof hairs slightly illuminated by the late-hour bulbs along the motel quads. They came in from the red-capped hills at sundown; and more than a few could see methamphetamine's presence around the dim corners of the cowboy Mecca. Its jaw-sucked imprint was burned into some employees who clean the motel rooms, women who rambled under eves, blabbering from acid-washed faces as they pushed carts though frigid wind and scattered snowflakes.

AS DUNNING'S SAGA played out, there were still some in Custer County who believed he could win his life back. Among them was Terry Hanson, who was planning a vigorous defense intended to destroy the prosecution's case by suppressing key pieces of evidence. And Hanson was far from alone in believing Dunning could be resurrected. With his solid build and brawny features, the fireman simply did not look the part of a ravaged meth addict. Methamphetamine often kills skin tissues and constricts blood vessels in the face. Some users in its grip eventually find the mirror becoming a reflective pool of weight loss, broken teeth, ground-down molars, diseased, retreating gum lines, rampant acne and facial cysts. The havoc meth plays on blood flow can also cause a crawling tingle in the nerve endings, prompting the user to pick open craters in their face with fingernails in an attempt to chase away the scarab movements scampering in their cuticles. Addicts pushing through extreme sleep deprivation or chemically cooked psychosis sometimes actually believe insects are twiddling through their skin, which can drive them to pick bigger, bloodier sores in their face as they try to force out the "meth mites."

Thanks to the efforts of a rancher named Tom Siebel, Montanans are generally among the most educated Americans in recognizing this gradual path to deformation. Siebel is both a computer software designer in California's Silicon Valley and 30-year range rider in the tough Montana countryside. While he may be a man who lives in two worlds, Siebel has a firm commitment to the land of the Big Sky. As methamphetamine began to spread its infection through Montana, Siebel's friends in law enforcement relayed tales of its disastrous, disproportionate impacts on crime, child abuse and the foster care system, especially in the most rural parts of the state. Siebel decided to get involved. He created the Montana Meth Project in 2005, a private foundation that took the same consumer marketing strategies Siebel had used to become a star in the California business world and applied those techniques to the mission of "un-selling meth to young people." The result has been an ongoing, privately funded media campaign that shows how physically horrifying the consequences of meth addiction can be. Hard-hitting, graphic and controversial, its billboards with real photographs of meth-mouth and sunken, corpse-like faces are spectacles that few teenagers can turn away from.

But Leonard Dunning did not look like those destroyed images. To many in Miles City, he was the man in row two of the fire department's portrait, standing in dark slacks and a blue shirt, shoulders raised and hands folded, an engraved silver badge gleaming on his chest. Some who knew Dunning warned about rushing to judgment. The former captain's supporters drew a picture of a man who was exceptionally generous with his time, having volunteered to help children with disabilities and serve as a referee for high school football games. There was also a good deal of talk that Dunning was one of the most compassionate, professional firefighters in the city. Such sentiments helped counter-balance the other talk swirling around Dunning's name, including rumors that before his arrest he was observed with large amounts of cash at different businesses in town. The question became murkier with every day leading up to the trial: Who was the real Leonard Dunning?

On February 12, 2010, just days after a breeding show had Main Street cluttered with steel cow pens and the snort of yearling bulls, Terry Hanson arrived at court for a hearing of motions. He had one mission: Cut the legs out from the People's case against Leonard Dunning. With his client present, Hanson questioned agents Dan Baker and Jeremy Waldo about seizing Dunning's garbage bags without a warrant. The garbage had been key in obtaining the court order to raid Dunning's house. Hanson argued that Dunning, who had stopped paying his garbage bill, considered the trash private property, since there was no reason to think unpaid sanitation workers would be coming for it. Hanson's theory was that the garbage

bags were not legally abandoned on the morning drug agents
had grabbed them. After putting forth his claim that the bags
remained Dunning's private property, Hanson quickly turned
his attention to the search warrant for his client's house. "The
search warrant, absent the fruits of this unconstitutional trash
dive on July 28, is deficient in establishing probable cause," he
told Day. "The concerned citizen information is all fine and
well, but it has to contain specifics, and anonymous tips have to
be corroborated ... by the time the search warrant was issued,
that information was stale. It was over three months old, and
nothing had come of that investigation as far as we know from
what's in the warrant application."

There it was, Dunning's whole defense: a suppression argument, an anti-cop tactic. There would be no explanation for the
drugs or the cash — simply an innocence by technicality claim.
Dunning must have known this would leave plenty of ammunition for anyone praying for his disgrace; and yet it stands to
reason the former captain could only defend his reputation if
he remained free. The "abandonment" strategy appeared to
be Dunning's best chance for escape. He watched his attorney
press on with it, referencing several examples of Montana case
law, including the infamous "Blue Chevy case," where a rul-
ing by Judge Day himself had gone against Hanson and then
been upheld by the state supreme court regarding what constituted legal abandonment of property. "That brings us to the
Blue 1993 Chevrolet case," Hanson declared. "That, of course,
is your case," he said to the judge, "and I argued that in the
Supreme Court, and the court determined that you were correct
and I was not correct."

Day quipped, "Sometimes they can be brilliant."

Without breaking a stride, Hanson submitted that the Blue Chevy case determined what constituted abandoned trash and that the circumstances in Dunning's case were vastly different. "These containers behind Dunnings' residence, while close to the alley, were actually on his property," Hanson affirmed. "I believe that law enforcement should know whether or not that property is placed for collection. I mean, where are we going to draw the line? They decide whether there is a bag in somebody's backyard, they run in and grab it? This must be garbage? Somewhere along the line, you have to draw the line."

Day appeared skeptical. "I'm not trying to be flippant about this at all," he responded. "It's very serious. I mean it to be that way: If it looks like garbage, it's in a place that garbage normally is, in a garbage can, in garbage bags, that it wouldn't appear to be garbage?"

Hanson offered a few carefully-tailored legal points, returning to his theme that the drug task force had perpetrated a grievous invasion against Dunning's right to privacy. When prosecutor Wyatt Glade countered that Dunning had taken no steps to establish an expectation of privacy, Hanson lamented to the courtroom, "What kind of state would we have if we had hundreds of thousands of our residents putting out 'no trespassing' signs up and down their alleys and all around their houses? It would be horrendous. And what kind of state would we have if everybody put up chain link fences? Pretty soon they're going to put up barbed wire on top of it. It's ridiculous."

"I've thought this over carefully," the judge told both attorneys. Dunning waited in silence. "I think the overriding factor here is whether there is an expectation of privacy evidenced by the defendant that society would recognize," Day went on.

"Those words, 'that society would recognize.' … there are trash cans in or very near the alley. They look like trash cans. They are in a trash can rack. They have trash bags in them. They are at least hard to see from the house, if not impossible to see … there are no fences. There are no gates. There are no lids. I mean, extra-tight lids or containers here. There is simply trash bags in open trash cans, it appears. I don't think society recognizes an expectation of privacy under those circumstances. And for that reason, I'm denying the motion to suppress."

And then it was over. The warrant for Dunning's house had survived. A jury would see all of the evidence in the case: the bags of methamphetamine, the bundle of cash, the residue-charred light bulbs. There would be no returning to the prestige of the firehouse, no wearing the silver badge again. There was only the one looming possibility: state prison. Worse yet, if the court believed Dunning's position as fire captain held him to a higher standard of conduct than the average Montanan, as courts have been known to do with law enforcement and political figures, then Dunning could very well find himself receiving the maximum penalty. In Dunning's case, the maximum exposure was two decades of incarceration in Cascade County, Dawson County or the Crossroads Correctional Center outside Shelby. The Siebel Foundation's war against meth was in full swing and Leonard Dunning was poised to feel the wrath of it, a poster child for Montana's growing frustration with the ugliness meth had wrought within its majestic borders.

The months passed. Roughnecks and rodeo men from around the high west flooded Miles City again for the 2010 Bucking Horse Sale. Its Friday was kicked off with the Mutton Bustin', small children looking egg-headed in their helmets as they clung to annoyed sheep that jounced through one corner of the arena. A Scottish bagpipe troop led the Saturday morning parade that followed. The kilted spectacle moved between the storefronts, their pipes filled with a rustic, weeping memory of the first Highland immigrants who had tamed the county with ranches and homesteads after the Indian wars. By June, some locals were honoring their roots by taking a 200-mile wagon train expedition out of Miles City, across the bumpy grasslands to Deadwood, South Dakota. This quest to relive the historic Miles City to Deadwood Trail made newspaper headlines across the state. Around the time the wagons headed out, Leonard Dunning put his signature on a document that would end his battle with Montana prosecutors.

"Do you notice, Mr. Leonard, that my signature doesn't appear on these documents anywhere?" Judge Day said as the former fire captain stood before him on July 2, 2010. "In other words, this is an agreement that you have reached with the state of Montana acting through Mr. Glade's office. I could impose the maximum penalty allowed by law."

"Yes, sir." Dunning responded. He then waited as prosecutor Wyatt Glade announced to the court that, in exchange for Dunning pleading nolo contendere—or, legally guilty without admitting guilt—to one count of felony possession of methamphetamine with intent to distribute by accountability and one count of felony possession of property subject to criminal forfeiture, the people would ask for a maximum penalty of no more than five years in state prison and a fine not to exceed $50,000. In addition, Dunning would enter a straight guilty plea of criminal possession of drug paraphernalia.

Day listened carefully before he turned to Dunning. "Do

you understand that the court treats a nolo contendere plea the way it would treat a guilty plea?" he probed. "They may be personally different, but they are legally the same ... Do you understand it's treated as a conviction?"

The words, "Yes, your honor," passed through the courtroom. Within minutes, Dunning allowed himself to be questioned on the record by his own attorney.

"The reason you are entering these pleas today is because you examined the evidence against you?" Hanson asked.

"Yes."

"And you discussed that evidence and the current charges with me, and we have decided that if you went to trial there's a likelihood that you would be found guilty?"

"There is a possibility of that," Dunning agreed.

"And you have decided that you do not want to go to trial, you want to enter these pleas today?"

"Yes," said Dunning.

Day soon made it official. "Based on those pleas of nolo contendere to Counts one and three," he said, "I find that the defendant is guilty as charged...and he's pled guilty to count four."

Miles City's best-known drug suspect had thrown himself on the mercy of the court. The move had saved Dunning the further humiliation of a media court carnival, but, in reality, the agreement offered only limited protection from spending time behind bars. Its terms reduced the penalty for his meth distribution charges from a worst-case scenario of twenty years in prison to a maximum of five. Yet pleading guilty to the other charges left Dunning to face a possible ten-and-a-half years of incarceration. The matter would be entirely up to Day.

AUGUST 31, 2010 was blue and sunny over the scattered sage-brush outside Miles City. Dunning approached the faded Art Deco stones of the Custer County Courthouse. Day entered the courtroom with a pre-sentence investigation from the county probation department, along with a sentencing recommendation from the district attorney.

"Mr. Dunning, would you like to say anything before the sentence is pronounced?" the judge inquired.

"Not at this time, your honor," Dunning said. "No, sir."

Glancing over the probation department's report, Day noted out loud that Dunning had no prior criminal history, many friends in the community and a number of special talents. "From the little bit that I know of you, I believe those are all true," the judge remarked. "But even despite that, you committed these crimes … so there is something that needs to be addressed, and this sentence is intended to address those issues and the reasons you are here—the reasons you are sitting in that chair by your attorney in a courtroom on a beautiful afternoon instead of being outside. And I think that you need to start addressing those issues."

Without much pause, Day announced that he was issuing Dunning a suspended sentence of three years in state prison, which was only suspended on the conditions he successfully complete three years of probation, pay $7,000 in fines and undergo a chemical dependency evaluation.

"You have a number of supporters, Mr. Dunning," Day observed, looking at the fallen firefighter. "You have a number of people who are on your side, who think that you are a person who is worthy of their letter of support … Your significant other is in the courtroom. She's obviously here in support of you.

Those are important things. It's important to the court to know you have people pulling for you out there. Many times people sit in your chair without anybody on that side of the courtroom. You have that support, but you will lose it if you fail in these conditions. If you fail, you will come back here and I will impose a sentence that very likely would involve prison time … This is your chance. This is your chance to show how this can work. You won't get a second chance. So make the best of it."

Leonard Dunning walked down the shallow cement steps of the courthouse. His days living in Miles City were over. His days saving lives were over; but his own life—the one that had hung in the balance exactly one year before—was still in his own hands. One hundred sixty miles south, a wagon train that had started in Custer County bumped over a long span of Wyoming prairie. Ahead of it, before the city of Deadwood, awaited the Black Hills of South Dakota, a jagged rise of towering pine trees that cast a thousand shadows the riders had yet to pass through.

CHAPTER 5

Jackson, California: June 13

MIKE COLLINS POUNDS the accelerator. The voice calling for backup over his radio belongs to a police officer in Sutter Creek, Jackson's sister city to the north. To Collins, it sounds like a fellow cop is approaching two burglary suspects caught in the act; and he's confronting them utterly alone. Mosquitoes are swarming as the Jackson cruiser drives under the bloodshot silhouette of a mine frame, ridges and rooftops below swept by a champagne curtain of light. The car moves through an intersection, past a white, plaster slum structure with rusty air units and bed sheets hung for drapes: Carrion eaves, cracked Spanish arches, its condemned walls flash by the veteran's eye in an instant. Radio traffic advises Collins that the policeman has his suspects cornered in a cemetery. By now, the cruiser has pushed through two staggered intersections to an upper gateway to Sutter Creek. For an instant Collins can see down the rolling vista to a basin of houses and yards a magazine once deemed "the city without crime."

IT'S ALL IN THE EYELIDS — the burglar's are low, ruby flaps of half-hung skin. Below them, two pupils shutter into postmortem windows, wobbling and wandering on the salmon-white glaze of his corneas. The eyes are vacant, deeply chiseled into a gaunt, shaven skull. The burglar's agitated. Trembling. He can barely speak. Moments before, he had no problems pattering to the Sutter Creek officer in front of him, even joking that the reason he and the emaciated woman at his side were spotted creeping out of garages was because they'd been taken by the carnal urge. Laughing, he'd quickly dropped the line that they were just looking for an impromptu place to satisfy it. But two black bags lay near a headstone, and Collins is watching as his fellow officer searches through them, discovering twenty-one stolen items hidden under knotted clothes and a bottle of Hennessy. The last thing the officer pulls out is a roll of toilet paper. Securing his gloves, he moves his fingers up inside its cylinder to discover a crystal pipe loaded with methamphetamine.

"That's insulin," the burglar assures everyone.

Handcuffs slide out of a leather sheath. The Sutter Creek officer moves in, but his suspect suddenly wants out of the graveyard at all costs. The wiry man locks his fists as a frail snare line rattles through his elbows. The much larger officer wrenches the burglar's forearms. The meth is good for one more push, a trapped tugging and some wordless defiance. Collins is ready to step in and help when the Sutter Creek officer, in one motion, forces his suspect down on the hood of the patrol car.

Collins cuffs the thin girl and leads her into his own vehicle. "Amador: Four-pol-four," he mumbles into his radio, "En route to CJ with one." The car drifts back from cemetery oak trees as flint-washed and cinereous as the headstones their leafless branches orbit over. Collins glances at the girl in his rearview. She's hardly impressive, as far as criminals go: Drawn, flushed, a weepy pink salamander shade bruising beneath the hopelessness in her eyes. Yep, Collins thinks, not much of a hardened criminal at all; and Mike Collins has seen his share of hardened criminals. Raised in the family of the Los Angeles Police Department, Collins' father was an officer who preached that the secret to surviving the most dangerous profession in America is knowing how to talk to people. And Collins inherited that gift. Stormless when he can afford to be, commanding when he needs to be, the Irish-descended beat cop has a knack for getting cooperation from the most indurate drug offenders through his plain, "no bullshit" manner of speaking to them. The Garden City Police Department in Idaho recognized his talents early on, promoting him to the most coveted of all law enforcement jobs, homicide detective. Collins worked three murders right out of the gate, including the brutal extermination of a female gas station attendant in April of 1981. Today, during late hours on his graveyard shifts, when his car's spotlight lances slowly over black stumps and darkened fields, Collins still thinks about Dixie Wilson soaked in blood. It's a permanent picture in the officer's head, the night two men wandered into her gas station, one staying behind the register as the other hauled Dixie into a small oil room. The perpetrator up front handled customers that roamed in. His partner sexually tortured Dixie during lulls in foot traffic. The two men eventually stabbed her thirty-six times before ending her nightmare with six bullets to the head. They grabbed $47 in cash out of the register before walking away from the woman's desecrated body. Detective Collins caught both of them. He put one on death row and the other in an Idaho state penitentiary for life; but, during soundless moments in a patrol car, the whipped, red droplets of Dixie's crime scene can find Mike Collins again, one of the few slayings he ever investigated that wasn't drug-related, one of the only acts of human degradation he ever confronted without a motive beyond sheer depravity.

By the late 1980s, Collins was working narcotics, executing high-level cocaine and heroin buys that took him from Boise to Salt Lake City and, in some cases, back to his hometown of Los Angeles. He helped surround Ryder moving trucks stuffed with bags of white powder. He used crowbars to bang open coffin-shaped crates packed with AK-47 rifles. He followed cars on surveillance details while speaking to helicopters that trailed high above. It was the proverbial big time; but Collins slowly began to want something different from the badge: He wanted to have laid-back dinners with his friends, to throw the squeaky toy for his dog, to watch a good Sunday NFL game. More than anything, he wanted to spend more time with his wife, Cathy. In 2002 he walked away from urban law enforcement altogether, finding the rewards were everything he hoped for. At the same time, the Jackson Police Department realized it had scored an experienced drug cop who quickly adapted his skill set to the city's methamphetamine problem. Collins was learning quickly that meth addiction made rural law enforcement harder than most city cops guessed, and the species of criminals running rough powder through the hills fed into tense encounters. One night in December of 2008, Collins caught a member of the Hells Angels preparing to burglarize an auto shop on Scottsdale Road. The Angel had a four-prong stun gun, a home-made blackjack and a cocked-and-loaded crossbow, all within easy reach of the driver's seat of his pickup. Collins was hardly surprised to discover that the five-time convicted felon was also transporting a bag of methamphetamine through the south end of the city. Collins managed to talk that suspect into handcuffs without drawing his .40-caliber; but he's pulled his piece plenty of other times in his nine years in Jackson. Christopher Jarod Stockton is proof enough. Collins has lifted his gun on The Giant twice now.

Though rural police work had its surprises, there are elements of it Collins has come to forever embrace. Officers typically have more time to investigate cases than their counterparts in larger agencies. They often get more breathing room to be genuinely sympathetic to victims and their families. For cops who care to get involved, there's plenty of face-to-face time with drug addicts trying to get clean, and occasionally opportunities to stop them from, in Collins' words, "seriously screwing up." Most small city police officers also develop unusually close bonds with residents, merchants and community leaders. And in the veteran's mind, there's something above even those privileges: Officers truly get to know troubled and at-risk youths. Sometimes they even get small chances to help them overcome the inner turmoil—that deep, inherited poverty of the spirit—so many in the rural underclass are born into. When people ask Mike Collins what it means to him to be a Jackson police officer, his answer is never long in coming. "It's pretty simple," he says, raising his eyebrows, "Out here, one cop can do a lot of good."

FIVE DAYS LATER, the weekly newspaper starts pelting doorsteps across Amador County. The burglar's deep-set, cindered eyes are featured in color on page eight. Though locals are becoming half-immune to reports of drug-related crimes in the Gold

Country, there's something noticeably different about this smudged 11 inches of newsprint. It's a prowler tale, a methamphetamine story; but its cemetery is not in West Point, River Pines, Jackson, Ione or San Andreas. Readers might have to look twice, but this is an article about the city of Sutter Creek. Even in the height of the Great Recession, Sutter Creek has remained a darling of the California travel media. Hailed as "the Jewel of the Mother Lode," *Sunset magazine* frequently showcases its Dickensian balconies and gingerbread gables, reveling in the tidy kaleidoscope of Victorian snapshots, the rare window to hardy Gilded Age dreams—a painted, polished five-and-dime tribute to lasting western elegance. Along with the town of Murphys forty miles south in Calaveras County, it's one of the region's top tourist attractions. And now, there are two long columns of text about desperate individuals stumbling around the most picturesque avenue in "the city without crime," hiding crystal meth in their grab bags as they burglarize addresses in broad daylight, all while the unsuspecting residents are home.

Todd Riebe glances at the online version of the headline with his smart phone. Moving in and out of an office crowded with files, the district attorney can imagine the wave of concern for property values that's hitting Sutter Creek this morning. Odds are the newspaper will be getting complaints from numerous real estate agents before the day is out. For his part, Riebe's mind is on a slew of pending cases, including a major investigation into fifty-two-year-old Victor Callahan, a man Riebe's preparing to charge with second-degree murder.

ON A SCORCHING July morning in 2009, Callahan was speeding down Highway 88 along tall humps of brass-baked grass near

Amador County's western border. The ranchlands fell around him in knuckled grades of frightening dryness—an arid harbor of yellow swells that intensified in the sun's early rays. Grazing heifers blurred by his Ford Taurus, their tough, ropy tails swinging through visible heat waves. Callahan's eyes drifted across a lone scarcely wooded hilltop. As his hand rocked on the steering wheel, the skin inside his left elbow was crinkling the crater of a fresh needle mark.

Five seconds later, Callahan's Ford became a gleaming, silver streak in the brightness. It veered across the double-yellow lines of the highway, crossing into oncoming traffic, sideswiping one car and then barreling head-on into a red Buick Lacrosse. Callahan's face was the last thing 84-year-old Ysauro Bernardo Lujan and his wife, 92-year-old Mildred Lujan, saw before the vehicles collided. The Lujans' hood snapped. Frosty blue webs spun and crawled up their windshield as the Buick's entire front end imploded. Ysauro felt the driver's side "A" pillar collapse. His ears were filled with the blare of metal tearing like paper. As the roar hit a crescendo, the dashboard gouged into Ysauro's body, cracking his ribs, crushing his pelvis and sending a transverse fracture up his sternum. The sounds reverberated and the dash continued to press inward. Ysauor's spleen split open. His bladder ruptured. Fluids began hemorrhaging into his abdomen.

Then silence.

Mildred looked out on the roadway to littered soil and a metal cattle fence peeking over shaggy weeds. She was motionless from a fractured spine. Her chest had slowed from deep, internal injuries. Mildred turned her eyes to her husband Ysauro, watching him take his last, lagging breath. Firefighters soon pulled her from the wreckage. She could feel the paramedics readying her battered body for an airlift across the valley. As they fastened straps around Mildred's skull, Ysauro was laid near the rear of the Buick, his medical board smashing down on the brittle amber grass with crushing finality. His eyes were peeled open. Firefighters moved a yellow tarp over his face.

Patrick Ong and Frank Peixoto of the California Highway Patrol soon approached the emergency responders attending to Callahan. One medic, a retired cop, told them he was seeing "objective indicators" of a drug roiling through Callahan's central nervous system. Ong looked his suspect over: Gauzy red trickles splintered on different parts of Callahan's dark flesh; and his small ribcage was laboring up and down, lurching painfully. Ong hunched over to study the man's dilated pupils. His gaze moved to the fresh, open needle mark on Callahan's left arm. Ong got eye-level with his suspect. "Sir, you're under arrest," he'd said, "on suspicion of driving under the influence of a controlled substance."

Callahan was rushed by helicopter to University of California, Davis Medical Center. Three weeks later, Ong and Peixoto got their hands on the results of his blood work. Any doubts were put to rest: Callahan had been under the influence of methamphetamine when he slammed into the Lujans. Ong made a personal visit to Ysauro's widow eight months later. The 25-year veteran investigator could see Mildred's body was mending, but the trauma of the collision had been seared into her mind as permanent scar tissue. Ong told Mildred he was sorry for what she had gone through. Mildred replied that she was still going through it—that she was reliving the sights and sounds of firing glass in her thoughts every day. A picture of Ysauro slowly taking his last breath was waiting when she closed her eyes. There was nothing she could do, she admitted to Ong, to stop seeing her husband die.

Ong and Peixoto forwarded their case to the Amador County District Attorney's Office. Now it belongs to Todd Riebe, who can only shake his head when he reflects on Callahan's long criminal history. Callahan has already been convicted of forcible rape in 1993, possession of methamphetamine in 2001, driving under the influence of alcohol or a controlled substance in 2006 and driving reckless under the influence of alcohol in 2009—the same year he took Ysauro's life. "If you go back far enough into his record, you find all kinds of stuff," Riebe remarks with tired disbelief, "like assault on a police officer."

Riebe puts the case with one of his best deputy attorneys, Steve Hermanson. Both men know other California counties have taken up a strategy of charging defendants who have killed someone with a car while under the influence with second-degree murder rather than vehicular manslaughter, especially in cases where the suspect has prior DUI convictions and is driving on a suspended license. That description fits Callahan to a tee. But the charge is risky, as no less than eight second-degree murder convictions are under appeal in the California Supreme Court. And yet, Callahan's record won't stay silent. The convictions tell the story of one man's blatant disregard for the will, rights and safety of anyone other than Victor Callahan; and if Riebe and Hermanson take a surgical approach to adding special allegations to each charge in front of them, a jury will get a pretty good idea of the life Callahan's chosen to live. The attorneys work the charges out. Count I: Second degree murder with a special allegation of a prior felony strike under the law, that being forcible rape, as well as a second allegation of causing great bodily injury to another victim. Count II: Gross vehicular manslaughter with a special allegation of prior drug offenses, including possession of methamphetamine. Count III: Driving under the influence of a controlled substance while causing great bodily injury, with a special allegation of suffering prior DUI convictions. Count IV: Driving on a suspended license with a special allegation of causing great bodily injury to elderly victims. The decision is made and Riebe and Hermanson are ready.

With Callahan's arraignment approaching, the prosecutors are going for second-degree murder in a way that will make his history ring.

TWO WEEKS PASS. The tale of burglars with broiled eyes stalking through houses in Sutter Creek begins to fade. When the newspaper hits doorsteps on July 9, one article is all over the city, all over the county and all over the western United States; and it's all because of Jackson Police detective Chris Rice. The headline reads, "Priceless blunder lands alleged drug dealer, gang member in jail." The arrest had its roots in an errant text message hurled through the universe of radio waves blinking over the mineshafts and tailing wheels on the landscape. At its heart, the message encapsulated the hopes and wishes of a handsome, dark-haired young man who was craving high-grade marijuana. Intending to get in touch with "a kid" he had recently met, the young man punched the words "Hey man, you got any dank?" into his phone and then pressed the send button. But the young man had been off by a few digits when he entered the new friend's number into his phone's contact list. Seconds later, around 2 a.m., the text lit up the cell phone that it had actually been sent to. An Amador County probation agent rolled over in bed, sleepily rising up to glance at the message. *Hey man, you got any dank?* The probation agent rolled her eyes in disbelief and slipped back under the covers. Early the next morning, she called Rice, who drove to her office.

"Who on earth would be stupid enough to do this?" the agent demanded.

Rice rubbed at the thin forks cracking up from his eyelids. The night before he had been working a major investigation into a member of the Hells Angels suspected of trafficking methamphetamine into Mule Creek State Prison. He was sleepless and slow moving, but he did have an answer. When the message was forwarded that morning, Rice punched the texter's phone number into a database. "I know this kid," he told the agent. He took the cell phone from her to study the original message. *Hey man, you got any dank?* A random thought began to percolate somewhere inside the detective's smooth, clean-shaven head. But no, Rice told himself. It couldn't work. Nothing in American law enforcement is ever that easy. And yet, within seconds, the Bumpkin was slowly and methodically working the keys of the probation agent's cell phone, replying to the text with an urgent dilemma of his own. "Sure, I've got plenty of smoke," he informed the young man. "But what I really need are OCs." After methamphetamine, OxyContin, or "OC," is the second highest priority for every narcotics agent in the Gold Country. Minutes later the phone Rice was holding pinged with light. Its screen heralded a new message from the texter that amounted to a simple proposition: Rice could meet him that afternoon and trade cash and marijuana for illegal Oxy-Contin pills.

"You didn't," Rice sighed out loud, shaking his head. "Come on, seriously?"

And the tale was about to get even better for the press: Not only had the young man contacted Jackson police through his own misadventure, and done most of the arrest work for them, he had also allegedly hatched a plot with another man to rob the guy bringing "the dank." When the local newspaper broke the plot of a nineteen-year-old who had alerted cops to his own drug deal and then supposedly tried to strong arm an undercover narcotics detective, media outlets across the western U.S. ran hard with it. From Sacramento, California, to Chicago, Illinois, stiff-haired, caked-up television reporters parroted one another, speaking into teleprompters with various half-gleeful inflections of the words, *Hey man, you got any dank?*

The original newspaper article is still on the break room table of the Jackson Police Department on the evening of July 14 as Rice straps on his gun belt. He walks outside to a patrol car, dropping in, hitting the gearshift and wheeling out onto the highway. It's 6 p.m. The sun is gradually cooling into a soft lilac afterglow that stains the rim of the hills. Rice takes his cruiser up North Main Street until it falls behind a car driving on the empty roadway. The detective runs the Nissan's license plate. Seconds later he throws a fast-changing flicker across a row of petite Victorians with matching bowed windows. The Nissan begins to slow. It cuts to a stop under two century-old olive trees.

Rising into an intermittent spray of crimson and blue, the Bumpkin checks a fake registration sticker on the Nissan's license plate before making contact with its driver. A pallid skullcap, nearly shaven to its skin, leisurely turns through the open window. The man's neck is a vine-woven scarf of tattoos that rise to his jaw line and the Fumanchu beard around his tense mouth. The webbed fresco sleeves both arms. It falls in runny, black ink veins from his mandible down his chest. Rice takes stock of the symbols: He makes out a litany of white-power insignias across the upper body and a bold swastika on the chest; but it's the image of the Norse god, Odin, on the man's neck that gets Rice's attention—an emblem worn by all members of the Peckerwood prison gang. For more than twenty-five years, the Peckerwoods have refined a combination of Klu Klux Klan mentality with the Hells Angels' bravado to evolve into an obscure but committed group of racist street terrorists. The main dividing line between the Peckerwoods and their spiritual cousins, the Aryan Brotherhood, has to do with the latter's creed that drugs ruin the purity of a white body. Peckerwoods hold no such qualms. Methamphetamine is a staple of the gang's culture outside prison walls. Cooking meth and selling it amounts to a huge source of revenue for the group, along with running motorcycle chop shops and selling illegal guns. Rice glances again at the God of War tattoo on the man's neck: In 2008, just two counties away, a Peckerwood named Brent Volarvitch was convicted of murdering a highway patrol officer during a routine traffic stop. Volarvitch was driving on County Road 96, blitzed on methamphetamine, when officer Andrew Stevens pulled him over. No sooner had Stevens approached the driver's door than the Peckerwood shot him in the face with a .357 revolver, killing him instantly. During Volarvitch's trial, attorneys argued the 22-year-old's brain was so whittled and ravaged by meth abuse that he shouldn't be held responsible for the officer's execution.

"I pulled you over because you've got a sticker that says

your registration's current," Rice tells the man through his driver's window, "but the registration's actually expired." As the words leave his mouth, Rice recognizes a woman sitting in the skinhead's passenger seat. They make eye contact. "Hi, Laurie," Rice says. The driver calmly hands his registration over, identifying himself as Nick Lamarra. "Lamarra?" Rice observes. "Are you still on parole?"

"I'm not on parole," the man answers in a slow voice. "I just have tattoos. You're thinking of my brother."

Rice motions to the back of the Nissan: "Step out so I can show you the tag."

The door opens and it gleams—the six-inch, unsheathed blade of a knife tucked in the pocket of the driver's door. Rice allows the man to climb out before reaching down to pull the knife from its hiding spot. "I'm just going to hold onto this until we're done," Rice says, "for safety reasons."

A quick look at the tag and the suspected Peckerwood is back in the Nissan, waiting for Rice to make his next move. The officer's eyes drift across the computer screen inside his patrol car. When Rice strolls toward the Nissan through the darkness, he directs his subject to get out. "I need you to start being honest with me," Rice tells the man. "Because I'm well aware that you're not Nick Lamarra. I just used my computer to pull up mug shots of both you and your brother. What's your real name?"

"Roger Lamarra," the man answers. Roger Thomas Lamarra: Convicted of grand theft and burglary, he's done seven years in state prison before hitting the Gold Country to become a grand czar of parole violations.

"Do you have any warrants?"

Lamarra shrugs. "I'm not sure." Rice steps behind him,

drawing the slender, tattooed wrists into a pair of double-locked handcuffs.

"You're on active parole," Rice says. "So I'm going to search the vehicle." An Amador County sheriff's cruiser glides to a stop under the leaning streetlights. A minute later, Rice and the deputy sheriff are raking their gloved hands through items strewn across the Nissan's cab. Rice looks up at Laurie, who's quietly standing away from the passenger door. She watches as Rice and the deputy find a prison-style boot knife—sharpened on both sides of the blade—concealed in the passenger door. Seconds later they find two baggies of methamphetamine. So here it is: two hidden blades within arm's reach, and plenty of crystal head-dust to jitter the hand that might reach for them. Rice knows that arresting either of these subjects won't make the national media. In fact, it won't even make the local paper that's back in the squad room by the coffee machine. But, most nights, this is the job. Methamphetamine works in silence. The officers who go after it walk up to dim car windows of the absolute unknown and take their chances.

Rice sits down in his cruiser and turns to Lamarra in the back seat. The suspected Peckerwood elects to waive his Miranda Rights. "Alright," Rice says. "Whose meth is it?"

"It's not Laurie's," the other admits. "I just picked her up. I know it's not hers."

"Whose is it?" Rice asks again.

Lamarra looks up. "Put it on me."

"It's yours?"

Nodding, Lamarra declares in a heavy drawl, "I'm just a dope fiend." Then he offers a quiet afterthought: "I must have forgot it was in there, because I usually don't carry it in my car."

Rice can always appreciate that moment when the lies finally end. Here's Lamarra, serving himself up for what he and Rice both know will likely be another stint in prison, all to make sure a girlfriend living under her own string of misdemeanor convictions doesn't take a hard felony on her sheet for his slip up. Big, bad Peckerwood? Maybe in the pen. But not here. Not tonight. Rice steers his patrol car out from under the olive trees. He drives silently along deadened windows toward the county jail, an honest man in his back seat.

CHAPTER 6
'Death by Meth'

BRANDY MATHIS MOSTLY remembers the phone calls. They came every single day, electrified by the voice of her brother, Travis, whose coy, easy smile beamed directly through the phone receiver. Travis was more than Brandy's younger sibling: He was the best friend she had. The phone calls were constant reminders that the two were always there for one another—each an inspiring, half-secret cornerstone of the other's world.

Brandy knows those phone calls will never come again.

For several years, Brandy has watched her mother Kim attempt to dredge meaning from the most acute torment that a woman can experience. The outlet for this mission is the ever-reaching power of the Internet, that vast chasm of cyberspace where, in some ways, Travis's relaxed gestures and signature grin still find life force through the changing glow. Kim believes that in a virtual world peopled by friends and strangers Travis continues to reach his hand out, to spin a caressing poem out of the cruelest violence, to offer an elegy that shows love itself to be the greatest cost of addiction, and the greatest engine for survival.

Kim's blog about Travis is called Death by Meth.

Travis Holappa, along with his sisters Brandy and April, grew up amidst the small towns in Minnesota's Iron Range. It's a land where the sight of massive steam shovels tearing ore from cratered pits is tempered by the beauty of dense, endless forests and more than a thousand lakes. Travis was uniquely handsome, with straight, raven hair and deep brown eyes. For most of his young life he was a skateboarding fanatic, a connoisseur of outdoor barbecues and a camping ringleader who loved sleeping on the lakeshores of northern Minnesota. When it came to friendship, Travis knew no boundaries: Popular or unpopular, athletic or studious, creative or common, Travis related to people walking every path of the harsh, sometimes frightening, landscape of adolescence. Refusing to believe in the trappings of labels, he found a certain comfort in knowing he himself wasn't hindered from experiencing life fully because of them. What various people saw in Travis was a magnetic sense of humor, which tended to culminate in harmless but memorable pranks. Travis also found himself an extended brother to more girls than just Brandy and April. His positive attitude, encouraging nature and habit of hugging led many female friends to consider him family.

By 2002, Travis was the proud father of two little girls. Parenthood was a good fit for his boundless energy. He loved taking his daughters out to play and teaching them about the world. Kim could tell that Travis was still close enough to his own childhood to know how to show his girls some serious fun.

That same year, not long after Travis turned twenty-two, Kim began to notice changes in him. He had been bouncing around the little cities on the Mesabi mining range, dividing his time between the hamlet of Eleveth, the forest-lined edges of Aurora, the bars in Gilbert and the former iron strike of

Virginia. At first the differences were subtle. Kim would call Travis's house to no answer. The few times Travis's girlfriend did pick up, Kim was told a vague story about her son being out of town for weeks at a time. During one visit to Minnesota, Kim spotted Travis hanging out on a street corner with men she didn't recognize. When she pulled up in her car, Travis appeared nervous, on edge. Travis was hardly recognizable by Kim's last visit to Minnesota before the summer of 2004: He looked thin; his hair was greasy; a thick, unkempt beard was growing across his gaunt face. "He looked like a little kid who'd been playing in the dirt," Kim would later recall. "I thought to myself, 'this isn't my son.'"

At the time, Kim had never heard of methamphetamine, a substance that held all three of her children in its grasp. Travis was the most deeply entwined in St. Louis County's meth world. Brandy was a bartender and only used meth to take the punishment off her routine drinking binges. She knew Travis was using too; but she didn't understand that he had been completely overtaken by it. Travis had been snorting lines for two years. By June of 2004, when he was living on Brandy's couch, he had graduated to "booting," or injecting, meth into his veins with a needle.

It is widely believed Travis also sold methamphetamine on the streets for an insomniac engine mechanic named Frank Miller. On June 15, 2004, Travis made the greatest mistake of his life. It was during the morning hours of an all-night meth party in Aurora that he stole Miller's truck. The truck had an ATV in the back, along with a bag full of methamphetamine and $14,000 in cash.

The police found Miller's truck abandoned in the woods four

days later. The mechanic was enraged to see it returned empty. Feeling guilty, Travis combed the forests between Aurora and Cotton in an effort to find Miller's other property. After a few days he located the ATV and returned it. Miller assaulted him during the exchange. Travis desperately continued his search for the missing bag of money. Meanwhile, rumors spread through St. Louis County that Miller was in heavy financial debt to Mexican drug cartel suppliers in Minneapolis.

Miller's growing problems and Travis's mistake came to a final intersection on the night of July 24. Inhaling wafts of crystal fog at a party in Aurora, Miller was alerted by friends that Travis had been spotted using meth at a get-together in Virginia. Miller was incensed. He sent a message to Travis through another addict who owed him money, Jason Anderson. The message Anderson gave Travis was simple: "Pay up." A phone call from Anderson later that night informed Travis that he needed to meet Miller at the Gladiator Bar to discuss the money that had vanished. Travis walked to the bar from a friend's house as Miller sat trembling in a meth-induced rage inside a Cadillac near the Gladiator. Anderson was next to him in the passenger seat. When Travis moved into view Anderson rushed out at him, punching him over and over. Neither Miller nor Anderson knew that Travis's brother-in-law, April's husband Adam, was watching from a car parked in the distance. According to Travis's family, Adam was also heavily involved with meth. Adam would later testify in court that he ran out toward the attack on Travis, coming face-to-face with Miller, who threatened, "Fuck it—I'll kill you right now." Adam testified that he then ran for his life.

Some members of the Holappa family have doubts that

Adam really tried to save Travis. What is known is that Miller was carrying a loaded pistol that night, which he used to force Travis into the back seat of the Cadillac. It is also clear Adam witnessed Miller and Anderson speeding his brother-in-law off into the darkness.

At five in the morning Brandy's phone rang. She had been up all night drowning herself in liquor, pulling the occasional white rail up her nostril. Her mind swam in an incoherent haze as Adam's voice rambled over the receiver. Brandy sank back into bed and drifted off again. Around 10 a.m., her consciousness fluttered up from the wasteland of her sheets. "I thought Adam's phone call was a dream," she would eventually admit to herself. "I had heard him trying to tell me something about Travis, but I didn't think it was real."

Brandy frantically called her brother-in-law, who broke the news that Travis had been kidnapped. Stunned and crying, Brandy dialed her mother. Six-and-a-half years have done nothing to make the phone call less surreal for Kim. "Why haven't you called the police?" she remembers shouting at Brandy. "Why haven't Adam and April called them?" It would be months before Kim came to know the level of sheer terror Frank Miller instilled in the addicts of the Mesabi Mining Range. "There was such an incredible amount of fear with everyone there," she says. "They thought that, if they called the authorities, they would be murdered by other people in the county's meth ring."

Travis's friends and family soon joined the Gilbert Police Department in search parties fanning across the wooded lakeshores. Kim flew in from Colorado determined to help find her son. Days after Travis was abducted, Adam had contact with

Miller by phone. A blunt message was sent to the family that Travis "wasn't coming home." Police arrested Jason Anderson the same day. No one seemed to know where Miller was hiding. By week's end, police discovered a car they believed Travis had been held captive in after being pulled from Miller's Cadillac. Cracking its trunk, a grim image began to materialize within seconds: duct tape, a belt, a broken watch, and blood and urine stains.

A detective made sure Kim understood that he was no longer handling a missing person's case—he was working a homicide. Kim tried to find her way through a long, numbing cloud by asking if Travis's body would ever be located. "It will probably turn up," she was told by an officer. "Fall is coming and hunters will be going all through the woods."

Kim flew home to Colorado and waited.

On August 2, police caught up with Miller.

With the lead suspect in custody, the search for Travis persisted. Brandy was now the driving force that willed the parties on. On August 14, *The Timberjay* newspaper ran a major story on Travis's disappearance. Veteran crime reporter Steve Foss captured the search with simple but excruciating detail: "Out on the warm calm water of the sprawling Whiteface Reservoir, boats carrying anglers drone by, vacationers are enjoying Jet Skis, and the occasional sailboat moves before the breeze. And all around the 5,600-acre reservoir's sand shores, swimmers wade and stroke. One of the swimmers is Brandy Peterson. But Peterson was not enjoying the day."

The media attention soon played into a nightmare for Brandy. The same fears that had paralyzed her from calling law enforcement in the moment she learned her brother was gone were realized when people from the St. Louis County meth world started sending death threats on behalf of Frank Miller. Brandy and her two small children went into hiding.

On September 2, a hunter from Minneapolis wandered down a deer path near the Whiteface River, stumbling upon what the wolves and insects had left of Travis Hoppola. Forensic pathologists helped detectives re-construct the final day of the 24-year-old's life. After Miller and Anderson had sped away from the Gladiator Bar, Travis was bound with duct tape, held captive in the trunk of a car for eighteen hours and periodically beaten and pistol-whipped. Miller, still high on methamphetamine, then led Travis into a lonely corner of the woods. Travis was forced onto his knees as Miller stood behind him, firing ten bullets into the back of his head.

For Brandy, it was piercing beyond words to imagine what Travis had felt when he lowered his knees to the leafy ground near the river, with Miller looming behind him. The dull throb of the unknown went dead in her shoulders. There was nothing but a permeating emptiness running through her. Methamphetamine took what was left of the young mother of two. Before the substance led Travis into the darkness of a car trunk, Brandy had been an on-and-off-again meth user. After the slaying, she gave into it completely. She began inhaling the drug on a daily basis. She would sit quietly at all-night meth parties, watching people smoke its gritty globs off tin foil, or suck it through blackened, hollowed light bulbs. The addicts worked on their crimes in front of her, passing around counterfeit dollar bills, forging bad checks, showing each other how to commit identity theft. Brandy observed them, often without mumbling a word, scribbling endlessly in her notebook as she let the stimulant dust through her sinuses. Brandy was convinced that meth helped her brain process what had happened to Travis. She sensed it was a protective filter for her anguish. Without methamphetamine, Brandy wanted to cry nearly every moment of the day and night. With the drug inside her, Brandy felt she could manage to breathe between the excruciating dimensions of a world that threatened to suffocate her to death at any moment.

While Brandy was coming apart, Kim was pursuing justice against Frank Miller and Jason Anderson. She followed as the detectives doggedly build their case. She learned how a prosecutor absorbs the forensic evidence of a crime scene and molds it into a courtroom presentation. From one end of the law enforcement line to the other, binders were filling with discovery evidence, all of which the St. Louis County District Attorney shared with Kim. Anderson eventually turned on Miller, agreeing to testify against the man who was Travis's main torturer and killer. Kim could sense the case becoming real. She battled the immense feelings of hopelessness by talking to prosecutors on the phone nearly every week. When possible, Kim flew out to Gilbert to discuss the case with them in person. She put as much energy as she could into making her son's case personal to the D.A.'s Office — to burn Travis's calm smile into their minds just as clearly as the savage signature of the crime that had extinguished it.

But the lead prosecutor handling The People vs. Frank Miller had a difficult task given that methamphetamine was so widely threaded through his case. A good number of the thirty-seven trial witnesses were meth users or addicts. The drug is known to cause brain inflammation and dementia-like memory issues. Some witnesses against Miller clearly had difficulty focusing. At times their stories were disconnected with the general timeline of the murder. Adam broke down in tears during his testimony; and Miller watched it all with cold eyes. Even when the most gruesome evidence was presented in court, the mechanic offered no hint of emotion besides the occasional smile or unexplained laugh.

In 2005, a jury found Miller guilty of kidnapping and first-degree murder. During his sentencing, Kim mustered the strength to look at him and say, "Travis was my gift from God. You took away that gift."

Miller was sentenced to life in prison.

Kim achieved what many victims of crimes never experience: A measure of justice. She knew nothing could bring Travis back, but there was still time to help bring Brandy back from the living death of methamphetamine addiction. Today, Brandy says she knew her life was unraveling. In April of 2006, she sent her youngest son to stay with Kim in Colorado while she tried to deal with the drug-induced tremors in her daily existence. After two months, she asked Kim to send her son back. Kim refused. "She knew I was having trouble taking care of my kids," Brandy remembers. "She didn't want to give him back unless I was clean. She told me to come out to her, and she would help me. I realized I had to. My mom had already lost Travis. I couldn't let her lose another child to meth."

On June 14, 2006, Brandy boarded an airplane with her other son. She was high on methamphetamine as she listened to the jetliner's wheels lurch up, its engine droning through the white cloud line toward Colorado. Kim was with Brandy every step of the way in the search for a job, a church and a new life with her children. Attending narcotics anonymous meetings, Brandy eventually met and married a recovering meth addict who had been clean for five years. By the end of the decade, she'd been sober almost the same amount of time. Brandy mostly credits Kim with giving her a new future. "I couldn't have done it without my mother," Brandy admits. "She was there when I needed her, at my very worst moment. Getting away from meth is an incredibly hard road to walk down, and even harder without the right support. My mom showed me it was fine to cry all night over Travis. Before that, I never wanted to cry. But you have to cry. You have to. It's such a big pain."

Kim spent plenty of her own nights in tears. She has experienced methamphetamine's collateral chaos on every level that a family member can. Having kids immersed in meth use showed Kim the frustration and betrayal inflicted on addicts' loved ones: Being constantly lied to; being manipulated for favors, being guilted for money; having belongings disappear. Kim is also acquainted with the stress of worrying for a grandchild's well being due to a child's chemical-dependent helplessness. Yet, while Kim can empathize with the heartache the average family goes through because of methamphetamine, the typical drug-affected family will never know the anguish Kim has confronted. The grisly kaleidoscope of Travis's final hours still turns through her thoughts at times. More directly, Kim's been handed her own life sentence—as sure and irreversible as Frank Miller's—an existence of second-guessing her presence in her son's life, her smallest decisions and observations prior to his death, her very value as a mother.

Knowing these feelings would never fully lift, Kim believed the only way to process them was with faith and honesty. She had always loved to express herself through writing. A friend suggested she channel that interest into creating a blog, an on-line memorial where anyone could encounter Travis and learn from his murder. Kim threw herself into research for the project. In a decade when all adjudicated newspapers put their stories on the web for free, Kim was able to read about every facet of methamphetamine in the farthest corners of the United States and Mexico. One story she encountered was that of Mary Haydal, whose popular, energetic daughter Cassie was killed by a meth-inflicted heart attack on a bathroom floor in Miles City, Montana. Like Kim, Mary was haunted by the thought of having missed warning signs of her child's addiction. She decided to fight back by taking Cassie's story public, becoming a highly visible figure in Montana's campaign against methamphetamine, traveling from one rural community to the next trying to protect other parents from the agony of burying a daughter or son. Kim could feel Mary's pain, as well as the pain she recognized in so many tales she encountered in her online search. Eventually, one single nightmarish image formed in Kim's mind that encapsulates all her thoughts about meth in America.

"I see rats spreading across a floor," Kim almost whispers. "To me, methamphetamine coming into a community is a stream of rats crawling into a small apartment, more and more creeping out of the walls, spreading into the corners, scurrying under the beds, until the infestation has taken over every inch of the room—just a space of diseased rats twisting around everywhere."

Kim's blog, "Death By Meth," is meant to be a glowing beacon that sheds light across those rats. Widely visited, the website connects Kim's personal devastation with resources, links to news articles and public heath information. Long before the site existed, Brandy watched numerous addicts in St. Louis County stop using methamphetamine after learning about

Travis's horrific ending; now Kim is getting signs of the same phenomenon on the national level, seeing emails and postings from recovering meth users who find solace in the lasting display of a mother's love.

A purpose can be sustaining; and yet Kim feels no moral victories can entirely relieve the puncture wound in her life. She still imagines Travis running around the baseball diamond in his Little League uniform, or walking into her kitchen, eight-years-old, trying so hard to impress her by dropping newly-learned vocabulary words into his observations. And always it's the smile that's in her mind's eye — so second nature, so full of joy. As a public figure, Kim can speak candidly, even clinically, about her son's murder. But in silent moments when she dwells on all the ways Travis could make her laugh or feel warm inside, the dynamic changes: her calm, resolute voice begins to choke with emotion. "Travis was my son," Kim says. "He was the only son I had. I loved him so much, and I still do."

CHAPTER 7

THE EYES ARE on him.

Calaveras County sheriff's detective Josh Crabtree puts a forensic kit into his Jeep. A face is staring from a nearby wall. Crabtree ignores it. The young investigator glances at a search warrant on his clipboard; but those eyes are still on him—a Neanderthal visage the size of a cannon and painted in the rubbed tones of a decaying peach. Its hair is a wild main of oyster straw, its eyebrows decrepit, its mustache bent into falling droops of pointed steal. Crabtree's attention stays on the warrant. Detective Sergeant Chris Villegas approaches, followed by a newspaper reporter. "I think we're ready," Crabtree says, and yanks a sweatshirt over his .40 caliber and the gold star hung around his neck. Villegas pulls a loose, gray hoodie over his own gun and shield.

Noticing the watery face, the reporter asks, "That's not supposed to be Mark Twain, is it?" Crabtree barely nods. "That's seriously pathetic," the reporter throws back, jacking an eyebrow. "My five-year-old nephew could have done a better Twain with finger paints."

For an instant, Crabtree's lips tighten before he admits in a low voice, "I think you should know—that Villegas painted that."

"No he didn't."

"Wasn't it a community mural?" Crabtree ponders, reaching for the driver's door. "Some project where the sheriff's department works with school kids?" Villegas climbs into the Jeep without answering. The journalist ducks into the back as the vehicle pulls onto the highway, rolling down the same bumpy quilt of flats and folds that a young Samuel Clemens once ventured through, back when he found a world of scraggy dirt roads and half-painted walls near leaning fences. Clemens had continued south to a grungy mining lounge on Jackass Hill where he penned "The Celebrated Jumping Frog of Calaveras County." That "villainous backwoods sketch," as its author always referred to it, secured Calaveras's place into the mythology of Mark Twain. Even today banners of the old trickster sway in the breeze and his silver-haired presence glowers from dusty road signs and spotted windows in every corner of the county.

The reporter hoists himself up between the driver and passenger seats: "Villegas, you didn't really paint that mural did you?"

"I think you should tell him how much work you put into that," Crabtree urges his partner. An awkward silence imbues the cab. Josh Crabtree's skills at jest are legendary within his department, and they're often his best armor against the disquieting sensations that come with holding the only job in America that makes a person the arbitrator between flesh-and-blood victims and ethereal concepts like justice and closure. Wearing a detective's star means being a human frontline against the anguish, loss, anger and helplessness of strangers. It is often more overwhelming in a small locale like Calaveras County, where an investigator can bet his pension that he'll be running into victims of crimes at the gas station, or the grocery store—victims wanting to talk, wanting to vent, desperately wanting answers where there sometimes are none. For his part, Crabtree attempts to vanquish the pressure through a hesitant smile and dry, ready-loaded doses of sarcasm.

But there are some aspects of Calaveras County that a sense of humor can no longer throw a light across. Many of its poorest residents live in daunting isolation. It's the type of vast openness that recently set the stage for a man having his door kicked in, his hands zipped-tied behind his back and his body pummeled until his internal organs started to bleed. The assailants vanished into the quiet countryside as Crabtree watched the man's shocked heart expire inside the emergency room of Mark Twain Hospital. A day later, the Calaveras County Sheriff's Department issued a statement acknowledging that the homicide was likely drug-related. The same sense of remoteness was on Crabtree's mind when he walked into a trailer in Mountain Ranch last July to find a woman lying in a bed that was spattered with wide, globs of blood. The back of her head was cracked open from her boyfriend forcing it all the way through, not one, but two, closed cabinet doors in the trailer's bathroom. Crabtree saw the grapefruit-sized holes where her skull had penetrated the solid pine. He stepped over the smeared slicks of red, and the dark excrement that had evacuated from the woman's lower half after she'd been kicked and strangled. This is isolation. The same half-desolate emptiness that empowers the area's meth culture: Calaveras County, along with Tuolumne County to the south, are territories for the Peckerwoods, the Aryan Skins and valley chapters of the Hells Angels. In the case of the Angels, it's been nearly forty years since they began tearing across the region's open highways, exuding hints of the outlaw mystique that once made them symbols of the American counterculture —that is, before the 1970s when members were increasingly convicted of drug dealing, gun running, pimping, extortion, tax evasion and murder. Similar cases are still being charged against members of the Hells Angels, and the FBI has identified the organization as having a major role in the sales of methamphetamine from California to the Midwest. Highway patrol officers in Tuolumne County suspect the hard-charging icons of running meth across the foot of Yosemite National Park, all the way to the quiet mining camp of Mokelumne Hill and up into remote mountainsides of West Point, the unspoken epicenter of Calaveras's meth world.

No one needs to tell Josh Crabtree what the Hells Angels are capable of. Six months ago, he was covering an afternoon patrol when dispatchers advised him of possible child abuse outside a local bar. Crabtree was confronting the child's mother outside when he heard the thunder of beer bottles detonating, followed by patrons rushing to the door, mustering "Fight! Fight!" He bolted inside. Trinkets and neon totems spun by his peripheral vision: Through a portal to the left, two Hells Angels were holding a big man by his arms while a third biker wearing the Death's Head named "Jack" was stabbing the man with a knife. The man broke free, tackling Jack onto the ground. The other Angels launched into a kicking frenzy with their boots. Jack was choking in a headlock, snarling and gasping, "I'll fucking stab you to death!"

Crabtree charged through a thermal lagoon of human shoulders. "415 Physical," he managed to get out over his radio. "Twenty inside. One stabbed." The site of a Calaveras sheriff's deputy did nothing to calm the chaos. One of the Hells Angels who was kicking the victim turned and pushed Crabtree backward onto the bystanders. Before the detective could plant his feet a second fight broke out behind him. Crabtree wrenched around. Decoy fight. A Hells Angel was already stepping into his path, grabbing him. "Backup now!" Crabtree shouted as he knocked the biker off his center. "Now!" The command stopped the Angel—but stopped him just as a frail, disembodied voice came rising over din, yelling, "He's got a knife!" Crabtree saw Jack's blade for the first time, switched-out and wheeling down on the big man, who was already bleeding from stab wounds. Crabtree lunged, drawing his .40 caliber. He brought the barrel up to Jack's forehead. His eyes were on the knife. His finger was pulling the trigger. Every millimeter of slack against the firing pin was gone. He was already envisioning the rose spittle from Jack's cranium that was about to shower the bar; and then a murmur in Crabtree's thoughts stopped his hand. If he hit Jack with a bullet, he told himself, there was no chance of making it out of the bar. He would get one shot off, maybe two, before the other gang members wrestled him down to the floor and took his gun. Crabtree sensed Jack's head trembling through the tip of his pistol.

The detective took a breath.

He grabbed Jack by the back of his Hells Angels' vest. "Drop it, now!" he yelled. In that instant, Crabtree noticed a black leather object go sliding across the floor of the bar: It was the sheaf to a knife. Jack's weapon was a folding blade. Crabtree was hit by the spine-clenching realization that, somewhere behind him, a Hells Angel had just pulled a long, fixed-blade knife. He pushed off Jack, stepping over the bleeding man on the floor as he dropped back for distance. His gun came up at all of the Angels. "Everyone else out of the bar!" he shouted.

Patrons went dodging by. Jack threw his blade down and Crabtree reached over to catch him by the vest again. He hauled his prisoner toward the front door. A Hells Angel stepped in front of him to block the path. "You're not leaving with him," the Angel advised.

The .40 caliber Glock ripped up and touched its barrel to the Angel's head. "Out of the way," Crabtree ordered, pressing its iron hard into frontal bone of the man's skull. The Angel stepped back. Crabtree hurried Jack to his patrol car, cuffing him and pushing him in. The boiler growl of two Harley-Davidson engines fired somewhere around a corner. Crabtree knew the tires were screeching straight for Highway 4. On the way to the county jail, Jack mumbled that he was so drunk he could not remember most of what had happened. Crabtree booked him on felony charges of assault with a deadly weapon, making criminal threats and attempted murder. But there was an unavoidable weakness in the case. None of the witnesses in the bar on that May afternoon, including the victim, were eager to testify against a card-carrying member of the Hells Angels. The Calaveras County District Attorney's Office eventually allowed Jack to plead guilty to one misdemeanor charge of brandishing a knife in a malicious fashion. He spent less than thirty days in the county jail.

It was the tensest episode of Crabtree's eight-year law enforcement career. Most deputies in the Calaveras Sheriff's Department blamed the Hells Angels' reputation for hauling methamphetamine through the area, and the historic tie that traffic gives them to the Gold Country, as the overall reasons the standoff had happened.

RAINDROPS DOT THE WINDSHIELD. "What did the FBI get out of the girl?" Villegas asks, scanning Crabtree's search warrant.

"Some agents came and talked to her," Crabtree answers. "But I don't think she gave them anything." *She* is the sadder half of a young couple that's been burglarizing homes in southern Calaveras County. The other part of the team is the hard piece, a short but tough little man who has already been convicted of felony assault and felony possession of methamphetamine. Both suspects are in custody now, and it's not lost on the girl that they were captured with a plethora of stolen items from numerous houses. The weight is too much. She recently broke down in front of Crabtree inside the jail and confessed that her life had been unraveling into prostitution, adding that she knew a number of other girls who were selling themselves to feed their meth addictions. "If you tell me who they are," Crabtree suggested, "maybe I can find a way to help these girls. Maybe we can get them to some place where they're safe." The prisoner reluctantly agreed, yet when Crabtree called the Sacramento office of the Federal Bureau of Investigation to San Andreas to probe the matter, conversation between his suspect and the agents was nonexistent. Too afraid, Crabtree knows. Too afraid to speak up on the meth world. The detective is pushing his burglary case forward. Now it's just a matter of executing a warrant on the house where the girl and her convict boyfriend were staying at the time of their grand crime spree. The warrant should end the case.

The Jeep cruises along lush, wet ground swells. The Calaveras ranches blow by in rough, dynamic craters of grass lightly erupting toward a far-flung ridge of oaks and greasewood. The cattlelands eventually give way to farms and apple groves, and it's then when the detectives pull into a driveway where two investigators from another law enforcement agency are waiting for them. The back-up cops are relatively silent men. They stand back as Crabtree and Villegas carefully try to find an open door into the house. "Got it," says Villegas. The four men take up positions around the doorframe. Villegas, with a dark beanie on his head that matches his goatee, is holding his badge in one hand and his Glock in the other. Crabtree yanks his gold star up from the collar of his sweatshirt so it falls over his chest. He pulls his gun, calling out, "Sheriff's department!" No answer. "Sheriff's department. Coming in."

The detectives spread out through the cold, dim ataxia of filth. Every table, counter and chair is piled in rank food or scraps of garbage. Towers of old newspapers spread across the den like the dusty skyline of a miniature city rising above an over-fouled, overflowing litter box, the contents of which are spilled onto the mildewed carpet hairs. Villegas moves down the hallway, checking doors.

"You want to go into their bedroom?" Crabtree asks his partner. "That's where everything's going to be." The two men round a corner with their guns out, Crabtree heading first into the living space that his burglar and the prostitute call home. The floor is a corpse yard of disassembled power tools, broken kitchen appliances and putrid, heaping piles of laundry. Crabtree doesn't need to search this indoor landfill for more than a second, because nearly every stolen item from his warrant is in plain view on the bed. He puts his gun away.

The two back-up investigators wander up behind Villegas. "Damn," one of them immediately blurts. "It smells like they pissed all over the floor?" Villegas nods, eyes watering as he covers his mouth. It came at once, that warm stench of fermented human discharge now penetrating the detectives' nasal cavities and simmering under their optic nerves. Villegas walks across the room to open a window. His long arm reaches up for the chain of a ceiling fan. The dirty, webbed fan blades begin lurching. A few feeble whoops. The smell suddenly doubles in potency.

"You just made it worse," Crabtree jabs. "From bad to unbearable. Thanks Villegas." But Crabtree is already blocking the smell out as he probes the bed top, the swiped electronics, the snatched power tools, the dozens of pieces of stolen jewelry. "This is probably everything *we're* here for," he observes.

Villegas circles the room while his partner continues the inventory. Near the sliding glass door, Villegas glances down into a large box filled with car stereos, black stingrays with comet tails of ripped frayed wires jutting out their backs. "Yeah, probably everything *we're* here for," he agrees. He walks to the north corner of room. His instincts hone in on a satchel half-hidden under a broken desk. Villegas suddenly turns to Crabtree. "Hey," he beckons. The other detective glances up from the latex gloves he's pulling on. "Check this out," Villegas says, coming over with the satchel yanked open to reveal bills of counterfeit money sliding to the zipper's edge.

Crabtree rips one of the fake bills up to his eyes. "That's a federal offense," he mutters before directing his attention back the pile of damp clothes.

The reporter comments that the piss aromas are hurting his head. Villegas shrugs. "Listen," he offers, "you don't have a bad meth house until you start rolling piles of laundry around and find dead, rotting animals underneath."

The reporter nods and then notices a sheet of paper on the

bed near the mounting collection of stolen items. He points at it. Villegas picks it up. "My Life on Drugs," the detective reads from the top of the page." He hands the poem over: *Stealing and lying, family home crying, / Money all gone, nothing to pawn, / fear and depression, compulsion, obsession. / God hears my prayer, let the connection be there. / Holes in my arms, burglar alarms. / Here comes the heat, cop car, back seat. / Handcuffs and jail, no O.R. or bail. / Feelings of impending doom, cheap motel room. / No spiritually, can't face reality. / Waiting to die, too afraid to try. / And saying all the while, I'm not in denial. / I just need a good reason to stop.* Villegas watches the reporter examine the poem for a long moment before shaking his head and tossing it aside.

Crabtree looks up. "Here's the missing jewelry." Gold and silver chains come boiling up in his hand. By now, the back-up detectives are standing in the middle of the room with their guns tucked away, looking down at Crabtree as he digs through a mess of sex toys and soiled female lingerie. "I can't believe I'm doing this," Crabtree says. "Just what I was hoping for when I got up this morning."

One of the back-up investigators looks at him: "Yeah, but you're doing such a good job."

Crabtree starts to crack a few signature jokes as his hands sink farther into the mound of objects from a sex worker's trade; he's getting smiles from the journalist and the other detectives; but, in truth, his thoughts are actually reeling the other direction. He was sincere about wanting to get the prostitute help. He was just as sincere about wanting to find a way to get her addict friends, who are selling themselves for meth, off the streets for good. His best plan would be to get them into a treatment center and safe house — the type of facility that his wife, Tammie, has helped run in Jackson for more than four years. Law enforcement officers and victims' advocates confront crime through different prisms; but for Josh and Tammie Crabtree, there is no retreating into the custom-built comfort of a single thought world. At night, Tammie sees the migraines and vexed frustration of her husband's caseload almost visibly wrapping around his skull; and before dinner is over, Josh Crabtree will hear about his wife's day, about her helping female assault victims get restraining orders, about her sitting next to rape victims in court as the rapist tries to menace the girl from the other side of the defendant's table. Josh Crabtree's task is to pursue criminals who think they won't be pursued. Tammie Crabtree's job is to battle the shock, trembling and tears those same types of individuals leave in their wake. Neither goal can be entirely checked at the door each night. At the very moment that Josh wades down through items used by a meth-addict prostitute burglarizing homes in Calaveras County, Tammie is across the county line in Amador, working at the women's safe house with several clients.

One of those victims is Betty, a woman who for the first instance in her life is trying to comprehend a future without violence. Betty has had relationships with men for more than twenty years and for all of that time she's gravitated toward individuals who would re-affirm her own self-loathing through physical aggression and emotional terrorism: They've been men who can sense a fractured self-image like a shark senses blood, men who get power over a woman by verbally flaying the same open wound and then actualizing it with bare knuckles on flesh. It is a bent mirror syndrome, for Betty truly thinks some deep, naked ugliness beneath her attractive exterior has so devalued her life that she is lucky if any man considers her his unconditional property. Tammie has seen women in this condition more times than she can count. But there is something else at play. The more Betty talks to her new friend, the more it becomes clear that force of rage is not the only weapon abusers have used to hold her down in an abyss of degradation. Alcohol and methamphetamine have also played a role. Betty is finally ready to admit that—at least for the moment. "My addictions really were a huge part of why I stayed," Betty tells Tammie. "If someone knows you have an addiction, it gives that person so many different ways to control you."

This was true of the relationship that finally brought Betty into the safe house. Her last boyfriend put her under a form of house arrest, and, when she finally summoned the courage to argue about it, he pummeled her so viciously that he collapsed her left lung and permanently paralyzed a section of her face. The world became a fuzzy blur of hospital beds and unknown visitors coming and going until things pulled into focus when Tammie and several other counselors from the safe house reached a hand out. Now it's been months. Betty claims that she won't go back to the man who disfigured her. Tammie's heart tells her not to hope: She's watched other women return to their abusers after being equally brutalized.

Another client Tammie's working with is a girl named Kelly, who's been at the safe house for a month.

Kelly is a methamphetamine addict; but she's far from the typical methamphetamine addict. At twenty-six years of age, she has straight, sable hair, a clear, dove complexion and classically beautiful features. Resilient genes and luck have so far kept her immune to the outward pocks and scars of hardcore meth abuse. But Kelly has inner scars, an awful connective tissue around her memories just as grisly as the Faces of Meth portraits seen on billboards across Montana. When Kelly was a child, her mother's drinking binges commenced with belittling her daughter before escalating to hitting her and spitting in her face. This oppression turned to terror during adult parties her mother hosted: Some of Kelly's earliest flashbacks are of being sexually toyed with by men inside her own home, presumably while Kelly's mother was in another room or passed out. Kelly does recall, with vivid nausea, being molested at the age of seven by an older woman that her mother had left her with. "My mom was the victim of sick, disgusting abuse by family members when she was young," Kelly explains to Tammie. "I feel like, since my mom was partly in denial—sometimes honest about it, sometimes falling back to hide it—that I became the target of her anger. And it's just sad she let that get in the way of protecting me. When I was a little older I would try to talk to my mom about my memories. She would act like she didn't believe me. She never wanted to deal with the molestation. If I brought it up, she would just take me to the mental health department, hoping they'd put me on medication. She was always trying to hide the stuff that happened to me."

By age sixteen, Kelly was smoking marijuana and dating older men. Neither development bothered her mother, though small arguments in the house still erupted into full-blown physical combat. Kelly was pregnant with her first child before her seventeenth birthday. "I think that was my way to getting my mother to stop hitting me," Kelly explains. "Turns out it was just the beginning. For me, violence started with my mom, but continued because I got into a pattern of choosing men that were just like her, men who would hit me and say cruel things." Kelly was a seventeen-year-old single mother when she first snorted methamphetamine. In the arms of the stimulant she found a euphoria that numbed her pain—an ever-present embrace that didn't run from her, or reject her, or leave her feeling small, battered and submissive. Kelly was working in San Andreas, getting drawn further into crystal meth addiction when she met the man who would take her to hell. Soon Kelly was pregnant again. She would sit smoking meth over the living bump in her belly, in full view of her son, as she watched her new boyfriend transform a small apartment into a clandestine laboratory. He was selling meth. He was inhaling meth. He was starting to beat Kelly during arguments. Methamphetamine was a dangerous enhancer to his temper. The drug fed and fueled his aggression while at the same time degenerating his grip on reality. He became suspicious, paranoid. He would have hallucinations that Kelly was speaking with other men—men who were not even real—and then he'd viciously whale on her with his fists.

"In terms of experiencing fear, I was so messed up that it really didn't matter to me," Kelly remembers with tears in her eyes. "That's not what I was scared of. I was scared of what he might say. At the time, I would have rather had him beat me then to have him tell something horrible, like that I'm a bad mother."

California Child Protective Services eventually took Kelly's son into protective custody. Months later, the meth cook that she was living with struck her so brutally that she went into premature labor. Kelly's child came into the world quivering at 3 pounds, 12 ounces. When Kelly's mother appeared at the hospital, it was not for support, but to announce that she was praying that the baby would die in order to teach all involved a lesson. The tiny infant fought for strength for forty-seven days in a special care unit. Forty-eight hours into her own stay at the hospital, Kelly was doing methamphetamine inside her room, snorting dust into her head and wondering about her critically frail child down the hall.

Kelly's baby remained in intensive care. She was pregnant again within days of coming home. Child Protective Services would ultimately intervene and take away both of these children fathered by the meth cook, who nearly shattered Kelly's jaw the afternoon he learned the kids had been rescued. In the coming weeks, the beatings got so painful that Kelly fled her tormentor into a new relationship. She had escaped the meth cook. She could not escape her own addiction. After a fourth child, a daughter, was born, Kelly fell to her lowest point: She found herself selling her body at the direction of a new boyfriend. Homeless with her daughter, she finally reached out for help. She was brought to meet Tammie Crabtree.

Kelly's been off methamphetamine for a few months now. Tammie's observed her new client brave weeks of intense therapy, trying to be receptive to the counselors' message that the beatings and the choking and the spitting in her face were not a penance brought on by Kelly's failure to read corrosive thoughts in the minds of her various abusers. Kelly claims she understands this. She tries to articulate different responses to Tammy's questions, suggesting she agrees that no woman writes a warrant for a man's violence through her own words and actions. Yet, just as Kelly is trying to stop blaming herself for the assaults, she's also trying to summon the courage to truly own the guilt associated with the mental abuse and dangerous neglect to which she willfully exposed all four of her children. It's difficult for Tammie to gauge how far along the road Kelly is to the stabbing experience of that revelation. Actions speak louder than words, as the tired adage goes; but words are always a start. So far, the words coming out of Kelly's mouth do suggest she's reaching a new, hideous clarity. "My oldest son saw some things he never should have seen because he was with me when I first got on meth," she admits to Tammy. "When I visit with him now, I realize that he behaves so good, and he's so smart and does so well in school. If he had stayed involved in the life I was living, he wouldn't have turned out that way. I know part of healing is learning that the way I was living wasn't the right way.... When my kids were first taken, I couldn't see that it was better for them to not be around me; but I know my that other children are safe now, because they're not around as I'm rolling out of bed at one o'clock, and there's not strange people around putting them in danger. I'll never let anything happen to my daughter now; and I never wanted to hurt my other kids either. I understand that today. I just wish that I could have understood it back then, because I want to be a family so bad."

It's another tearful voice that will stay embedded in Tammie Crabtree's memory, and, by extension, in Josh Crabtree's consciousness. Playing the hardened detective may work for temporary stress relief; but when your best friend spends her days facing the disbelief and disappointment that comes with daring to hope for others, a jaded edge is only hard on the outside. The job still means something. The job has to mean something.

JOSH SLOWLY GATHERS all of the missing items from the burglaries into a single box, the dense cloud of urine still thick in the air. "I think we're done," he says to Villegas as he stands up. Turning to the reporter, he glances at the box and adds, "Do you like that? These addicts break into people's houses and steal their shit. We break into their house and steal it back." It's a small victory for the afternoon. The five men walk back outside to their vehicles. "You know what?" Josh remarks as his entourage climbs into the Jeep. "I still can't believe you said that about the mural Villegas painted."

Just before steering the unmarked unit out toward the highway, Josh Crabtree sends a text message to his wife, asking how her day is going.

CHAPTER 8
Trail of Tears

JIM LANGFORD LOOKS out at dark treetops glossing along the Chattahoochee River. His window is fixed nine stories above Interstate 75, a massive byway that snakes from the north countryside into the jagged-nail silhouette of downtown Atlanta. Langford's view is a wash of viridian on gray—the maze of Georgia's integrated capital—sweeping parks and forests that pour in thick moats around concrete and civilization. But on an afternoon in late February of 2011, Langford's eyes are pulled across the wavy braille board in his window toward Atlanta's suburb of Lilburn, the site of a recent horror.

It was a Thursday, just before 4 p.m., when flames suddenly erupted through the light blue Victorian-style home on Spring Mill Drive near the lawns of Mountain Park. Black smoke poured from a dormer as two teenage boys pulled off of 5 Fork Trickum Road to investigate. The young men encountered a woman outside screaming that her three small children—a four-year-old boy, a three-year-old boy and an eighteen-month-old baby girl—were trapped inside. The teens quickly attempted to brave the front door, only to be cut off by a dense curtain of heat. Running around the house, one of the young men managed to boost the other onto a corner of the roof. The rescuer scrambled over the shingles, entered a window, ran through the smoke and flames and found the children. By now a carpenter had pulled over and was using his ladder to get the other teenage boy onto the roof. Together, the young men began passing the unconscious little ones through the window as the structure grew hotter. The first Gwinnett County firefighter to respond entered a frantic scene unfolding: Two severely-burned children were laid out on the ground, motionless, while the teenagers pulled the third child off of the roof. Arriving fire personnel also noticed an unidentified man in his early thirties, with a rose-singed face, spraying the erupting flames with a garden hose. The man soon disappeared. Firefighters and paramedics steadily worked to save the unresponsive children. Advance life support efforts went under way as all three were rushed to area trauma centers. "They were covered in extreme burns and they weren't moving," Gwinnett County Fire Captain Tommy Rutledge would later explain. "We knew the outcome was going to be grim."

Early the next morning, Gwinnett police announced that the unassuming house on Spring Mill Drive was actually a major laboratory for cooking methamphetamine, and that arson investigators had already determined the residence likely exploded because of trouble during the cooking process. Gwinnett County Police Captain Jake Smith told reporters that, inside, his officers had found 9 pounds of liquid meth, 1 pound of "finished" meth, 4 pounds of incinerated powder meth, along with $192,000 in cash stuffed in a wall. Smith added that the mother of the three children was charged with trafficking methamphetamine. The alleged operator of the lab, the man with the singed face, was missing and wanted for drug trafficking, arson and three counts of murder. By that time, all of Atlanta was learning that the two toddlers and their eighteen-month-old infant sister had perished from the fire.

Three weeks after the incident, Langford again glances out his window toward the edge of Gwinnett County as he speaks to a journalist about the three children who were lost. His steady tone drops into a hushed, half-choked cadence when he recalls first hearing of the explosion. For just an instant, the three deaths seem to linger in every element of Langford's gentlemanly mannerisms, his deep-set gaze, the calming drawl of his voice. If Langford is taking the incident hard, it is because he's at the forefront of the battle to keep methamphetamine from tearing Georgia's social fabric to pieces. He's deep in the fight, but he himself is not a police official, nor a prosecutor or politician. Langford is a public strategist and southern intellectual now tasked with exposing the hurricane of despair meth is churning across the only state he's ever called home. He inherited that task in 2010 when he was named Executive Director of the Georgia Meth Project. Today, in Langford's mind, one of the organization's main goals needs to be putting human faces on the most innocent causalities in the state's meth epidemic: small, defenseless children.

This mission for Georgia's future began five years before and two thousand miles away as Tom Siebel's Montana Meth Project pushed its startling media campaign onto billboards and televisions across the high west. By 2011, Montana was experiencing a 63 percent reduction in teen meth use, according to the Montana Office of Public Education, and a 62 percent drop in meth-related crime, as cited by a report from The

Montana Attorney General's Office. Many in law enforcement, education and civic leadership felt Siebel had made a palpable difference. But Siebel's role in the fight wasn't over: Just as he loves ranching and range-riding, friends say he also has an affinity for quail hunting, which occasionally brings him to sprawling plantations of the Peach State. In 2008, it brought him into the company of then-Georgia Attorney General Thurbert E. Baker. It was through Baker that Siebel learned more about Georgia's growing problems with meth; and that Baker thought it needed the type of hard-hitting prevention initiative that was rippling under the Big Sky. Siebel agreed to meet with prominent businessmen from around the state to discuss the possibility of creating The Georgia Meth Project. When the afternoon finally arrived, the idea of helping law enforcement seriously challenge methamphetamine's stranglehold over Georgia was nearly killed by varying degrees of enthusiasm. But Lee Shaw, a philanthropist and business leader known throughout Atlanta, saw the gravity of the situation. Shaw's hometown of Catersville may be a durable, historically rich piece of northwest Georgia, but it's also one of many communities in the south hit hard by meth-related crime. Stopping Siebel after the meeting, Shaw offered a personal guarantee that he could make the Georgia Meth Project a reality.

As the building blocks began to fall into place, Shaw and Baker understood they needed the right person to steer the new endeavor, someone with a deep understanding of Georgia's cultural and economic complexities; and someone who knew how to get results. They turned to Jim Langford. Years ago, Langford had graduated from the University of Georgia with his sights set on becoming a journalist. The path his life would ultimately take included working as a political staffer, an archeologist, a corporate executive, expert in historic restoration and Georgia's most recognized figure in land conservation and green-space sustainability. By 2009, Langford's accomplishments ranged from founding a non-profit group protecting sensitive archaeological sites, to converting $40 million worth of urban blight around Atlanta into fresh, open parkland. He was arguably one of the busiest men in Georgia. But Langford had reasons to hear Shaw and Baker out; and like Shaw, one of those reasons was a love for his childhood home.

Gordon County, Georgia, is a tree-swept breadth of farms, rivers and creeks: As a boy, Langford grew up fascinated by its mementoes of history and that long, cloaked specter of the Civil War that haunts its white oaks and every edge of its hardwood. Sherman was here. He left an anamnesis of blood on the landscape—a vague, nameless feeling that still shades a lane in the north part of the county off Battlefield Parkway. The path winds along the brush, turning beneath a cluster of fine, raw-boned pine trees before coasting into the beauty of a glen. The Resaca Confederate Cemetery's arch awaits in a poignant vision: A rise of Stone Mountain Granite blackened by the soot of passing seasons, stitched in dark moss and bathed in bleak emerald curtains of grime. The soil beyond is adorned in streams of grass and colonnades of sycamores and sweet gum trees spread through a star field of bantam, foot-high marbles. Old. Wordless. These pearly nubs jut up like broken teeth scattered over clay and weathered, ginger quilts of petals. It was May of 1864 that the Battle of Resaca engulfed a field just across the road, leaving blue and gray-clad corpses strewn in the open air. It's said a young woman from Calhoun was initially responsible for getting the rebel dead buried along these Georgia pines, in one of the first official confederate cemeteries in the South.

Down the road are more signs of Gordon County's legacy in the apologue of America. Only six miles from Resaca's mosaic of forgotten graves is New Echota, a serene expanse of fields cleared in the woods, a space marking the former capital of the Cherokee Nation. It was from New Echota that the Cherokee legislature won an epic legal battle against forced relocation in the United States Supreme Court in 1831. It was also at New Echota, after being betrayed by a sitting American president four years later, that the tribe's forced exodus was sealed. The Trail of Tears Highway sways north from New Echota up into the city of Chatsworth in Murray County, where a tall, colonial-style courthouse with its tusk-like pillars looms over Main Street's bricks and the soft curves of the Appalachian Mountains. These eighteen miles of roadway represent the first few hours of torture that would eventually cost nearly six thousand Cherokee people their lives. Most of the victims were children.

Langford got his first taste of archeology at the New Echota excavation 1969, working alongside seasoned professionals in a quest to restore one of the Cherokee homeland's greatest treasures. He would return to Gordon County over the years, driving alongside the pines and open meadows that make it a gem of slow-moving Southern life. But by the 1990s, Langford was starting to sense methamphetamine's presence during his visits home. Stark, generational poverty has been with Gordon and Murray counties since they were founded, and, in some cases, that privation led families into distilling moonshine, which Langford remembers as "sort of lurking around different corners" when he was a child, though few in the middle class talked about it. Moonshining was a mode of life that existed on the periphery, a tradition that took the spirit of living free to its most rebellious and extreme manifestations in the coves of Appalachia. Illegally distilling "White Lightening" has, and still does, often involve dumping contaminates into pristine creeks and rivers. The finished product is strongly associated with major illness, blindness and even death. Nevertheless, moonshine remained a powerful seduction in the South for decades. Some residents of Gordon County think that methamphetamine crept into the remnants of the moonshine families first, leaching onto a ready-made culture of isolation, boredom and hopelessness. Regardless of its origin, the Southern meth epidemic began infecting longtime farming and merchant families from Calhoun to the Tennessee state line—to the point where a number of the generational farms that Langford had grown up near were being repossessed by banks because the children who had inherited the property were unraveling from their addictions to meth.

"Gordon County was always a self-sustaining, ideal little community with great interpersonal relationships," Langford explains. "But I could see what meth was doing to it. I would catch the ravaged faces around my hometown of Calhoun. It was a problem that was really threatening everything there." Langford's family eventually took in a foster child whose parents were involved in crime due to meth. The issue then became even more personal. When Baker and Shaw approached him in 2009, Langford bowed out of several enterprises to take the helm of the Georgia Meth Project.

GMP workers began collecting data from across Georgia. By 2011, the board of directors was reviewing the most extensive summary of findings on methamphetamines ever gleaned from the state's schools, law enforcement and social agencies. The study revealed that the Georgia Bureau of Investigations was able to identify a 96 percent increase in meth-related crimes in the year 2009 alone. In 2010, Georgia's Family Dependency Treatment Courts ranked methamphetamine as the top substance impacting the state's drug courts, trumped only by alcohol. Alarming figures also emerged around the region where Langford grew up: Whitefield and Murray counties, Gordon's neighbors, were ranked among the hardest-hit counties for individuals seeking treatment for meth addiction. Worst yet, responding to the Georgia Meth Project's survey, the state Department of Family and Children Services reported that 85 percent of cases in Murray County where children were placed into foster homes involved methamphetamine. A startled Langford called a magistrate judge in his hometown of Calhoun—the Honorable Suzanne Hutchinson—and was told that methamphetamine factored into nearly all of the child deprivation cases that came through her court.

Langford and his colleagues put out an invitation for young people across Georgia who had been hurt by methamphetamine to share their stories. The messages came fast. "My house was a mess," remembered fourteen-year-old Whitney, whose mother and father were self-imploding meth addicts. "My parents were either awake for days on end, or sleeping for days. When I was eight-years-old, I was taken away from my parents. I lived with my grandparents for about four years. My sister ended up in foster homes. She ran away from multiple houses, moved all over. I didn't even see her once for almost three years ... My brother wet the bed until he was ten because of being pulled away from my parents so young … Although it is the past, the memory will always be there, and it will scar me for life."

Much like Whitney, thirteen-year-old Margaret could also recall how her parents' decline into methamphetamine abuse was heralded by basic failures in their daily routine. Suddenly her mother and father were unable to put meals on the table. They stopped getting their children to school on time. Margaret watched their existence become a perpetual cycle of begging for cash from her grandparents. And then came fear, chased by uncontrollable anger. "My parents would lock themselves in the bathroom and shoot meth," Margaret said. "I was a younger kid, and didn't really understand what was going on; but I knew it wasn't normal or good … My dad started hitting my mom, my little brother and I."

Seventeen-year-old Quinn shared similar memories. Authorities took Quinn away from her meth-addicted father when she was nine-years-old. Quinn's letter to the GMP described how her father eventually stalked her down and assaulted her grandmother in front of her.

Mary Reames, a fifteen-year-old who contacted the GMP, outlined the relationship between her mother snorting meth and the violence that often followed. "She didn't have a house," Mary Reames said of her mother, "so we'd be at a motel, or her friends' place. They'd be in another room for hours saying, 'We're talking about grown people stuff.' She would smile to her friends, lock the door and I wouldn't see them for the rest of the night. … I remember when my mom was coming down off meth, if I didn't breathe right, she'd smack me. She would hit me all the time. Once I didn't do something she said and she picked me up by my neck, so that I couldn't touch the floor. Then she threw me down."

One of the most unforgettable submissions came from Gwynne, a nineteen-year-old living in Dawsonville, a town of just seven hundred people. "My parents were on meth for six years," Gwynne wrote. "Soon, we lost everything. We had to move into this house that had holes in the floors. It had a toilet that never flushed. I mean it was just horrible …. We would get off the bus and my mom would be waiting for us, so that she could leave my little brother with me. She would stay gone days at a time. Then we moved to another trailer. That was even worse because the whole trailer park was on meth. We had people coming up into my bedroom at 3 a.m., waking me up to see if I had cigarettes or meth. There was one guy—he always came off as weird to me—and then one night, it was 4 a.m., and, as usual, my parents were not home. He came into my bedroom: I woke up to feeling my pants being pulled down. I told him to stop. I cried and pleaded; but he never did. He just said, 'Let me get what I want. There has to be some use for you.' He raped me three times in that one night. Out of all that I had went through, that was it. That was the end of the line for me. My parents were never there for me or my siblings. Because of them, I was raped three times in one night—and no one was there to hear my screams."

The Georgia Meth Project has used these testimonials to expose the swath of invisible pain methamphetamine is cutting through the South. More than anything, it is that very invisibility that's engulfing the state's children in dangerous and heartbreaking circumstances. While a place like Gordon County can take comfort in having one of the lowest violent crime rates in northwest Georgia, the transgressions that happen behind closed doors—the child abuse, the constant crimes of omission—which are spawned by meth are affronts to every value Gordon's community holds dear. A person keenly aware of this is Gordon County Juvenile Court Administrator Teresa Rice. In 2010, Rice noted that illegal drug use was either a primary or secondary factor in every child deprivation case she reviewed. "Drugs are part of just about every family we deal with," Rice will tell anyone who wants to know. "The families may come to us at the court for another reason, but, once you get into their cases, you find the drugs. A lot of it's methamphetamine."

Rice works closely with Judge Hutchinson, and the two are often forced to watch the same stories wrench through the county's legal system. When Hutchinson is compelled to remove a child from a parent's custody due to abuse or dangerous neglect, she does everything in her power to place that young one with a responsible relative rather than in foster care. The people of Gordon County put a strong emphasis on family connections. It's not uncommon for Hutchinson and Rice to discover that a meth addict's family is willing to "step up for the kids"—brothers, sisters, aunts, uncles and grandparents who are committed to offering stability to a child while their parent faces treatment or incarceration. Despite the family bonds in Gordon County, nearly half of the children involved in deprivation cases end up in foster care.

For many in the U.S., the term foster care invokes stigma, judgment and its own images of possible abuse; but from Hutchinson's perspective, the foster care numbers in her jurisdiction can be viewed just as easily as a badge of compassion for Gordon County as it can an indictment. "I know a lot of local foster care families," the judge is quick to point out. "I'm constantly amazed that there are people willing to open their homes up like that. These are some of the few resources that we have when it comes to the meth problem. Those small town values are the very reason that I chose to make this place my home and raise my children here. For the most part, people know the faces they're passing on the sidewalk. That breeds values that create a sense of accountability, an atmosphere where people have to ask themselves, 'Is my conduct an improvement or detriment to my friends and neighbors.' I don't think you find that in the cities. Here in Gordon County, if I'm having a problem in my court, I can always call someone, like a local teacher or business owner, and ask for help. There's never been a case when I've reached out for assistance for something happening in the courtroom and someone's said 'no.' If anything, they're usually scrambling to do anything they can to make the situation better. I believe it's because they have a deep commitment to this community."

While Gordon County may be blessed with families willing to quietly do their part in fighting meth's catastrophic effect on children, that involvement usually comes with an emotional price: Georgia law typically allows parents in deprivation cases opportunities to regain custody of their children. Family members and foster parents trying to protect children can be forced to watch an addict get another chance, fall back into his or her habit and further hurt their child, creating a thicker fiber of scar tissue swollen around the victim's mind-set. "Unfortunately, it's pretty common to see the same parents end up in court all over again," Rice acknowledges. "We'll have cases where a meth user has gotten their kids back because it looks like their addiction problems are behind them. Then it starts all over again. The judge understands the parent may backslide; but, after the third time, permanent custody is usually granted to a relative. The parent still has the option of petitioning the court later on, but that usually only happens after they hit rock bottom."

For the children at the center of deprivation cases, custody cycles and the trends of methamphetamine addiction often form a powerful, crippling theater of disruption. In the former Cherokee capital, it's the Gordon County Sheriff's Office and the Calhoun Police Department that are largely charged with trying to find these drug-endangered kids. Like most law enforcement agencies across Georgia, they are also the main line of defense in stopping Mexican drug cartels from trafficking the stimulant into rural areas. The federal government's 2005 crackdown on ephedrine may have caused the moonshine-like meth labs of Gordon, Murray and Whitfield counties to vanish, but, within three years, Mexican cartels had filled the vacuum, establishing their own laboratories in Georgia, while moving constant quantities of the drug from their distribution hub in Atlanta. When Gordon County Sheriff Mitch Ralston was elected in 2008, his top priority was adapting his department to the new and changing meth world. Ralston directed deputies to shift focus from low-level drug offenders to the cartel middlemen who are dealing in the region.

"In Gordon County, there are few families that don't know someone that's been affected by meth," says Gordon County Chief Deputy Robert Paris. "We've tried to put all our resources into targeting the organizations smuggling meth into the area. When you start tracking the firearms and electronics that have been traded for methamphetamine, it's clear that it's all Mexican cartel meth that's here now. We haven't had a real lab found in Gordon in two years."

This phenomenon has compelled the Georgia Meth Project to start making the analogy that meth is to the city of Atlanta what cocaine was to the city of Miami in the 1980s and 1990s—a glaring locus point for cartel activity that appears to be providing the lower southern United States with the bulk of its meth supply. It's an image of a tsunami, as Langford puts it: A wave of addiction that rolls out from cooking operations and stash houses in the state's largest city, cascading into the remote, rural country-sides, until it peaks, and then draws back into Atlanta's upscale suburbs, to places like Lilburn, where the three small children were just burned to death in a meth lab fire.

In many ways the tragedy perfectly illustrates the nexus between Mexican cartel operations in Atlanta and the rugged, wooded countryside of the state. The mother of the dead children—charged as an accomplice to the cartel operation that extinguished their lives—had just moved to Lilburn from Gordon County three months before. The woman's family members still live in Calhoun, some working at a carpet factory on the outskirts of the city. On Feb. 23, authorities took the children's mother on the two-hour drive from her jail cell in Atlanta to a picturesque cemetery in Whitfield County, some twenty miles from Calhoun. Newspaper reporter Josh Green from the *Gwinnett Daily Post* made the trip as well. He described the funeral for his readers: "[The mother] and more than 100 family members mourned at a Dalton graveside Wednesday as sun dissipated afternoon clouds, and beige earth was shoveled atop tiny, white caskets. Two brothers, ages three and four, lay stacked atop each other, their eighteen-month-old sister beside them."

Word slowly began to spread that the trinity of departed souls had grown up in Gordon. Their early conceptions of the world were forged by emaciated pines, by a Cherokee statue guarding the county library, by beaten red, white and blue ball caps flashed from the windows of passing pickup trucks. They died in a city; but their story was partly a Gordon County story, partly a rural story. And, as for Jim Langford, one of Gordon's more noted sons, his mind constantly goes back to those first-hand accounts that flooded into the Georgia Meth Project a year ago. They keep him up at night, because he knows that each letter represents a crime that a child is experiencing somewhere at that very moment. "They're terrifying," Langford warns. "And they're real, with no editing from us. They're what twelve and thirteen-year-olds are telling us they've gone through—everything from rape to types of abuse that will shock the daylights out of you. They show just how much children are constantly suffering because of meth. And they are hard for people to read. I won't read them before I go to bed. They're horrifying and depressing."

CHAPTER 9

West Point, California, January 18

CALAVERAS COUNTY SHERIFF'S Detective Josh Crabtree steps near the barn where the gunfight erupted. His eyes move over the scene with a bleached, red glow welded to the sides of sleepless pupils. There's a tension in his spine. Hurled bits of a patrol car's windshield flash in the tall grass and clovers. Crabtree knows the shell casings have all been lifted from the soil, zipped and stored in evidence bags in a cold cement locker back in San Andreas. Now there is only the mutilated mud under his boots, ravaged tire tracks that confirm the shooting was spontaneous—a blinding instance of smoke, thunder and cellular reaction. But there's also another truth written on the ground, a narrative woven through old garbage, oil bottles and spades of termite-tasted wood debris: Josh Crabtree has felt this day coming for a long time now.

Twenty-one hours ago, sheriff's deputies Kevin Stevens and Josh Shemensky launched a new special enforcement team on this north slope of Calaveras. A map in their squad room marks the region with "hot spots," yellow grids that move down the paper on a warped turn of remote villages: West Point, population 700; Rail Road Flat, population 500; Wilseyville, population 450. Despite its lack of residents, names from the area are permanently engraved in at least one facet of American history. It was in Wilseyville, between 1983 and 1985, that Leonard Lake and Charles Ng committed the acts that would brand them the most depraved serial killers to ever use California as a hunting ground. Lake and Ng kidnapped entire families and brought them to Lake's isolated compound on Blue Mountain Road. There, they slaughtered the husbands before raping, torturing and murdering the wives. They killed at least two infant babies, whose captive mothers were filmed begging to know where they were. The Calaveras Sheriff's Department would later find thirteen corpses and 45 pounds of charred, unidentified bone fragments on the property, making for a suspected death toll of twenty-five people. After a quarter of a century, the legacy of Blue Mountain Road is never far from the thoughts of some in the southern Gold Country. When the word Wilseyville, or even West Point, comes up in conversation, longtime residents still fight off a visual of the cinderblock bunker Lake and Ng used to torture their victims. Though a judge long ago ordered the bunker destroyed, the house remains at the end of an empty country road, its driveway blocked by a crude rebar gate sitting at the mouth of a lightless tunnel of trees that eventually bends into the woods' abyss. Some Calaveras deputies claim it's the most soundless section of forest they have ever visited.

Today, a cloud of hardship still hangs over the county's north hills. The boom-and-bust timber industry busted for good in the late 1980s—leaving poverty, unemployment and family-wide, generational methamphetamine abuse plaguing the citizens who remained. In 2010, 84 percent of the children attending West

Point Elementary School qualified for free or reduced lunch. Ten minutes up the mountain, at Rail Road Flat Elementary, that number was 88 percent. Teachers at both schools struggle to reach the poorly dressed, underfed children that meth addicts bring through their doors. Even having a handful of neglected little ones in a class can make teaching all the students a second priority. And the dwellings of such children are clearly visible on the outskirts of the towns, where pallid, dirt-dusted houses and spider-hole trailers with tarps on their roofs stand by countless, wasted car frames. To the Calaveras County Sheriff's Department, the meth culture that exists here appears permanently entrenched. In the last twelve months, deputies have arrested a parolee-at-large in Rail Road Flat for child endangerment and possession of methamphetamine, as well as nabbing two fugitives from justice in West Point, brought in on warrants for robbery, criminal threats, false imprisonment and possession of meth. The deputies also raided a meth lab in Rail Road Flat that was stocked with chemical toxins and illegal firearm ammunition. Last fall, an argument between three men standing on West Point's main street culminated in a knife assault that left one of them clutching blood. The year ended with Calaveras Sheriff's SWAT pinning down Jakob Main at gunpoint, after he dived out of the window of a house in Rail Road Flat. Main was wanted for drug violations, auto theft, shattering a man's arm with a baseball bat and allegedly trying to stab the same victim in the neck with a screwdriver.

This was the patrol beat Stevens and Shemensky were working on January 17, 2011. Their Special Enforcement Team was tasked with combating the slough of felonies becoming so common around the villages. The deputies were in full uniform when they rolled their Ford Crown Victoria out of West Point, southbound onto Highway 26. A few miles beyond the orchards they caught sight of a 1991 Volkswagen Passat parked in front of a narrow road. Stevens looked at its grimy windshield and saw a mountain man's eyes glaring back at him: The leathery face was more alert than a coyote, looking ahead with a blank snarl under the cave-top of a bone hard, ragged brow. The stranger's hand came up for a slight wave.

The deputies looked at each other. "He's up to no good," Stevens observed.

"I know," Shemensky said, moving the steering wheel to turn the patrol car around. "Something's not right." The Volkswagen suddenly accelerated off the gravel onto the highway, cutting over a dusty span of asphalt as it tore onto Rail Road Flat Road. Shemensky hit the gas. The deputies caught up. Ahead, they noticed a long barn spread like a sickly white coffin under the tree line. The Volkswagen circled around it at full speed. A second elapsed. The deputies broke off the roadway. Another second went by. The patrol car convulsed on a rocky section of earth ahead of the building. A third second passed. Stevens moved his hand down to his holster as the chipped, ashen planks came rushing into his peripheral vision. The fourth second came: The patrol car slapped through a fan of hanging pine branches on the corner of the barn—and then the mountain man was running straight at them with a 12-gauge shotgun.

Stevens internalized the figure: He saw it dashing through the shade and sunlight as it raised the shotgun up; his consciousness dilated into a tunnel around the long, steel barrel. And then there was no more barn; no more eclipsing pines; no crimson, muddy banks littered with brush and stump skeletons. There was only the barrel—and those hard, black and hollow eyes of the mountain man. "He's got a gun!" Stevens heard himself shout. The windshield exploded. A scalding wave of smoke and glass blew by the sides of the deputies' faces. Stevens leveled his .40 caliber at the mountain man and pulled the trigger. Shemensky brought his gun up, too. Sound in the patrol car slipped into a deafening vortex. Taming his breath, Stevens focused on his ambusher. He felt the shells ejecting from his pistol, round after round, beating through the patrol car's glass. Pain threaded down his ears. The cab was a resonating chamber of fire.

The mountain man retreated through a hail of bullets with his shotgun held over his head. He made a running dive for the Volkswagen. The deputies kept shooting. Stevens was on his thirteenth round. Shemensky was on his eleventh. Their target made his way out of the car, violently barreling into the trees, still holding his gun.

The long, crooked fork of a branch was pressing against Stevens' door. "Back up," he told his partner through a moaning roar in his skull. "Back up." Shemensky threw the car in reverse, one hand on the wheel, the other manning his pistol. The deputies broke out. Stevens covered Shemensky while he pulled an AR 15 rifle out of the trunk. Both men had been temporarily struck deaf. Using hand signs to communicate with each other, they took up firing positions that would stop anyone coming out of the barn.

PATROL CARS IN TWO counties slowed down as a message came over the radio: "All units, be advised, officer-involved shooting in Rail Road Flat. One subject fired at deputies. Multiple shots exchanged. Information pending."

Lights began to flash. Calaveras units went racing from different sectors of the hills toward West Point. The Amador County Sheriff's Office sent three of its own cars over the northeast river crossing while the Jackson Police Department kept a unit near the south river bridge, in case the suspect had made it to another vehicle and was escaping through nearby Mokelumne Hill. Several moments later, a second transmission came over the radio. "All Amador units, be advised," a dispatcher said, "Detective Crabtree is code three from his house to Rail Road Flat."

Josh Crabtree was at home when the call went out. He charged through his front door, making sure his SWAT gear was in his Jeep before wrenching the ignition to life.

Stevens and Shemensky had been alone for more than thirty-five minutes when sheriff's deputies began screeching into a nearby turnout. A K-9 officer from Amador eventually helped Crabtree and a few deputies clear the barn. When it was obvious that the mountain man had left through the forest, captains and sergeants began preparing for a manhunt. A search of the Volkswagen yielded a prescription pill bottle with the name Richard Kenneth Cooper typed plainly on its label.

Richard Cooper made his first impression on Calaveras County law enforcement in 1998, when he threw a savage beating on his then-wife and threatened to murder her with a knife, screaming, "I'll kill you bitch—right here in front of the kids!" The deputy who arrested Cooper also found him to be in possession of numerous stolen items. Cooper was sent to prison and, in October of that year, a correctional employee sent a letter to Calaveras Superior Court stating Cooper was trying to handle his anger by participating in narcotics anonymous. Cooper was a free man by 2003, though his propensity for mixing drugs and violence remained dangerously intact. Calaveras sheriff's deputies soon arrested him for assaulting a new girlfriend, who said he had punched her more than thirty times in the course of twelve months. When Cooper was taken into custody, deputies found him in possession of an illegal biker weapon and numerous hypodermic needles for shooting methamphetamine. Just hours before the gunfight ignited behind the barn, Cooper had been visiting a friend who's a convicted burglar and convicted methamphetamine dealer. That witness would later admit that Cooper was in a rage and looking to get even with another West Point meth user —a man Cooper assumed was trying to get close to his girlfriend, who herself has been arrested for felony child abuse, burglary and being under the influence of methamphetamine. The witness had also mentioned that Cooper expected his target would be driving down Highway 26 around the same time deputies Stevens and Shemensky first encountered the mountain man along the side of the road.

Crabtree was not yet aware of Cooper's criminal history as he looked into the peppered wreck that had been a department squad car. All that was clear was that the first round the mountain man fired had come within 2 inches of taking off Shemensky's head.

SWAT members were mustering along a creek bridge at the bottom of Rail Road Flat Road. Crabtree and Deputy Tyler Houston were strapping on body armor when they noticed a woman nervously watching them from a rock across the highway. Crabtree headed over to her. "What are you doing here?"

"I'm worried about Stephen," the woman answered.

"Stephen Gommeringer?"

The woman nodded. Every law enforcement officer in Calaveras County knows Stephen Gommeringer, whose last drug conviction in 2007 was for possession of methamphetamine and possession of a crystal meth pipe in a house on a thickly wooded slope of June Avenue. Despite spotty court supervision, Calaveras detectives have testified that Gommeringer's house remains "a popular place for probationers and parolees to hide out." Crabtree knew that house was not a quarter of a mile from the barn where the gunfight had just erupted.

"Why would you be worried about Gommeringer?" Crabtree demanded. "Is someone in the house with him?" The woman tensed up. "Is someone else in that damn house?" The woman's mouth wouldn't move, but the answer was scrawled through every inch of her weathered face. "Who's in the house?" the detective repeated.

"Rick Cooper," the woman finally said.

SWAT Commander Chris Huett was at an upper staging area when he was told about possible intelligence on the mountain man's location. Huett only had five SWAT members on scene, not including Stevens who, despite being deaf, exhausted and bleeding from glass cuts, was asking to see the confrontation to its end. A captain told Stevens to sit tight. The senior deputy felt a pang under his ribs that was worse than the throbbing in his eardrums as he watched his fellow SWAT members heading out to face the mountain man without him.

A WALL OF THIN, shaggy ferns made the dwelling nearly invisible from the road. The SWAT van's engine was killed. One by one, five men clad in camouflage slipped into the wild blankets of foliage on the hillside. Three officers crept past a deck to the northeast corner of the house. Their assault weapons were now covering the front door and the east side window. Crabtree and Houston approached an open sliding glass door on the structure's west side. Passing a back window, Crabtree caught Gommeringer in his sights. "Sheriff's department!" he shouted, taking up a position next to Houston. "Come out with your hands where we can see them."

"I'm heading out," Gommeringer quickly answered, shaken. "I am. I'm coming. Don't shoot me."

"Come out slow," Crabtree warned. A diminutive man moved into view. He stepped out, trembling, toward the officers. "Is the guy we're looking for in here?" Crabtree asked quietly.

"Yes."

"Where is he?"

"In the back—in the bathroom."

Crabtree and Houston trained their AR 15s through the sliding glass door into the house's kitchen and living room. They took aim at a blind corner leading to the back. "Come out," Crabtree ordered. "Now."

There was a bleating sound through the old wall panels. "I'm coming out," a voice said. "I have my hands up." Richard Kenneth Cooper suddenly materialized, shirtless, wearing blue jeans and suspenders. The instant he came into view the SWAT officers noticed the barrel of a shotgun resting on an armchair a few feet away. The laser sights cut into the center of Cooper's chest. They tightened their fingers, ready to send an array of .223 rounds into the target's heart and lungs. Cooper did not move for the barrel. He was directed onto the ground.

"Are you hurt? Houston asked, reaching for a pair of handcuffs.

"No," Cooper tossed back in a grizzled cough. "They didn't hit me. Are they o.k.?"

Cooper was brought down to Huett, muttering, "I fucked up, man I fucked up." The SWAT commander started frisking him and snatched a 12-gauge shotgun round from one of the suspect's pockets. Crabtree looked at the ammunition. "You're under arrest," he told Cooper, and then drummed through the Miranda rights. "So," he said after the quick recital, "what the hell happened down there?" Cooper went stone silent. The detective drilled him with a litany of questions. There was no response. Crabtree rubbed his temple. Staring out at the familiar trees and trails that snaked through this section of the mountainside, his thoughts slipped back to another case he has been working on for weeks. Alex Michael Anderson—a well-meaning, but troubled, fifteen-year-old boy from West Point missing since November. Probing the disappearance, Crabtree's already discovered that Alex was getting hooked on methamphetamine and spending time at the most infamous crank houses between the remote villages.

Alex first left home out of a sense of chivalry, determined to protect a young girlfriend who had fled her family life. He'd been independent since he was young; but once away from the guidance of his mother, Alex's warm and emotional nature made him a target. In a sense, methamphetamine's shadow had been stalking Alex for years. His estranged father was a long-time addict who also lived in West Point. Alex had watched the man wither and die from numerous health issues, a vigil that left him despondent and sometimes angry. Alex's mother put him in counseling, and, for while, the teenager appeared to flourish. He immersed himself in studying animals, building chicken coops, gathering snakes and rescuing wounded wildlife he encountered on his many hikes. One day most of West Point saw him riding his bicycle through town with a shaking, abandoned fawn wrapped protectively in the folds of his hoodie. Adults began to notice that Alex had a special gift with animals. West Point's health clinic closed in 2010. Alex's counseling abruptly ended. By the time he'd run off with his girlfriend, he was sinking back into unresolved grief over his father's death. Looking for traces of the parent he'd lost, Alex began visiting his father's meth addict friends in the area, most of whom lived along the same wooded paths and trails that Alex loved to explore. Through it all, Alex would still visit his mother, popping out of the forest at random moments to spend time with her, always tipping his hat like a gentleman to kiss her forehead before heading out the door again. Whenever he paused, his mother would kiss him back on both his eyes. In their last conversation, Alex's mother begged him to move away from West Point with her, escaping the pain, memories and the constant specter of methamphetamine. Alex raised his fine, strong eyebrows up high and shot his mom an expression that suggested he was seriously contemplating it; and then he tromped outside, wandering down a broken trail, possibly to discuss the idea of leaving with others in the local meth world.

He has not been seen since.

As the detective assigned to Alex's seven-week dissapearance, Crabtree's been systematically confronting West Point's meth addicts. No need to panic, several of Alex's much older adult "friends" have assured him. The teenager is the ultimate outdoorsman. Everyone knows he loves hiking and fishing and that his favorite pastime is to spend entire days alone in the wilderness. He's versed in all the hidden trails that connect the creeks and ravines. His head is a virtual map of every cabin, shelter and summerhouse spread through the northern woods. The portrait of Alex is true; but Crabtree is sure it couldn't account for forty-nine days without a sighting of the teen. One trail Alex often frequented leads right to the house of Steve Gommringer, who has appeared to be genuinely concerned about the boy vanishing. Alex not only spent time with Gommringer, he was also known to spend time with Cooper's meth-dealing friend, Cooper's girlfriend and, occasionally, Cooper himself.

Now, waiting for his captured suspect to offer some truth about the shooting at the barn, Crabtree had glanced at the rickety deck clinging to Gommringer's house and got a cold feeling under his skin. "Let me ask you this," Crabtree questioned his suspect. "Where is Alex Anderson?"

Cooper tipped his head back and then shook it with a mocking crack in his voice: "That kid's fucking dead."

SUNLIGHT SWINGS IN FORKS through the pines as Crabtree wanders behind the barn. He has been named the lead investigator in Cooper's attempted murder case. It's 11:35 a.m. Crabtree's had less than three hours of sleep. There's not one wrinkle in his heavy, tan slacks, or his black polo shirt with the embroidered star on the chest, but the detective is moving like he's in the clothes of a man who's been hit by a freight train. His primary interviews are completed, and they included a bizarre conversation with Cooper, after his capture, on the way to Mark Twain Hospital. Crabtree had noticed blood smeared on his suspect's forearm and left thigh. "I thought you weren't hurt," he asked. "Why are you bleeding?"

Cooper looked over: "It happened while I was running away."

Having documented Cooper's statements, the detective is now taking in the crime scene again with a fresh set of eyes. Is it different from other scenes he's had or helped other detectives work? There was Michael Thompson in 2009 — shot seven times by Calaveras detectives after struggling with them in a meth-fueled rage. There was Michael Fogelstrom, living in a suspected drug house in north San Andreas when men forced their way through the door with a loaded pistol and beat him to death, creating a homicide case that's been open since July. And, of course, there's the brutal acts of violence Jakob Main is suspected of committing. Crabtree is both an investigator in those cases and one of the SWAT members who caught Main at the end of an assault rifle. And now, here the detective stands — a few months away from county leaders slashing his department's budget, sidelining more patrol vehicles, denying more enforcement equipment and mailing out layoff notices to eight sworn deputies who attempt to patrol this very region. Crabtree's eyes look over rotted pallets and the mess of roofing shingles until his focus pauses at a dented hot water heater embedded in the mud. A shred of windshield glass sparkles under it. Two inches, the detective tells himself. The blast came 2 inches from Shemensky's head. "How long have we been saying things were getting out of control out here?" Crabtree asks, turning to the deputy. "How long have we been trying to make people understand that we have to be seriously going after these guys; because they think they can do anything they want in this place?" He lets his breath settle again. "No one listened," he adds with his eyes swinging back down to the tire-scorched ground. "Now they're are going to have to listen."

They walk out into the shaded glen where the mountain man first fled after the shooting, tracking his path. With every brittle snap of leaves dissolving under Crabtree's boots, his mind flies back to photographs of Alex Anderson—and then the sound of Cooper grumbling, "That kid's fucking dead." The detective knows there was nothing in Cooper's tone to implicate himself in the disappearance, though the off-handed words might carry the full authority of the entire mountain meth world, a sign that every cook, dealer and addict from Red Corral to Sheep Ranch believes, or knows, that something has happened to the boy.

Returning to the barn, the detective pauses at its splintered door. His knuckles push it open. He enters a dim sanctuary of webs and animal refuse. He probes the litter with his flashlight as the deputy steps inside. "I grew up on the other side of the river, in Amador," Crabtree tells the deputy. "My uncle used to take me to this barn when I was a kid."

"It's been here a long time."

Crabtree straightens up under the lace of webs. "It was full of bricks back then," he mentions off-handedly. "People used to come by and grab them for things." His eyes are transfixed on the endless mess of torn boxes, aluminum and motor parts. "Now, I'm just wondering if anything of Alexander Anderson's is in here."

They step back into the sunlight. "I've got to drive up Bald Mountain Road to check for stolen generators and property that's been burg'd," the deputy says. "Supposedly, there's a mine shaft next to a house that we emptied last week. The missing stuff from my case might be down the shaft." The deputy pauses, and then adds, "Yesterday a real estate agent noticed a man moving around inside the place; but we arrested everyone who was living there. They should still be in custody."

"I'll back you on that," Crabtree replies, not feeling his breath slow as he adds, "besides, at this point, we should be checking every mine shaft out here for Alex."

The marked SUV and Crabtree's undercover unit pull back onto the roadway, cruising down the hill to Highway 26. Ten minutes later they reach the far side of West Point to turn down Bald Mountain Road. The house waits in a perfect stillness under the pines. Branches coil down on its rust-speckled tin roof, throwing a leopard wash of shadows on its thin bay window and the high, narrow dormer. Crabtree jumps out and connects a .40 caliber assault weapon to a strap around his neck. The deputy draws her sidearm before the two officers begin to move around the property, stepping slowly down a grade to check two sheds that are all but falling into a thicket. "You can see why they'd be drawn to this place—free reign of the woods," Crabtree observes after clearing the main perimeter.

"House was built in the 1800s," the deputy responds with a glance along a web-laced trough clinging to the structure's eves. "But I don't see anything resembling a mine shaft out there."

"Doesn't look like it."

"Head out?"

Crabtree acknowledges the question by unstrapping his assault rifle. Opening the back of his Jeep, his tired movements grind to a stop. "Listen," he says as he looks over to the deputy. "You need to help me put the pressure on everybody on this road—our addicts, our parolees, our frequent flyers—all of them," he vents with an energy rising in his voice. "I'm making it known that we're going to be on them. It's going to be nothing but heat, until someone starts talking about Alexander Anderson." The deputy nods. Crabtree's eyes span a ragged section of brush near the driveway and then the dark shade and shadows beyond in the pines. "Right now," he says, putting his gun down, "Alex is the top priority."

THE STORY OF THE West Point gun battle had played out on television sets throughout northern California on the evening of January 17. The word "ambush" was stressed by anchormen—the phrase "deputies wounded" pushed hard by on-scene reporters. But when Richard Kenneth Cooper is arraigned for attempted murder in Calaveras County Superior Court two days later, the room is virtually empty, save for one newspaper journalist and several face-furled, sun-hardened mountain dwellers who watch from the back row. Cooper is led out in chains and a blood-red jumpsuit. Dropping lazily down into a chair, he throws a head nod to acknowledge to his acquaintances in the back. He smirks while his rap sheet, which goes back to the early 1970s, is read out loud into the special circumstances of his attempted murder charge. At one point he cocks an exaggerated eyebrow at a burglary conviction from Sonoma County that he can't remember—and then shrugs.

The following Monday, January 24, Crabtree is at home when he hears 911 dispatchers alert his department that something resembling a human body has been sighted in the woods outside of West Point. The detective walks calmly out to his Jeep. He drives through West Point, turning onto Bald Mountain Road, passing the trailers, the tireless cars, a half-built Miwok round house, before he hits his signal at a private road. He stops at the same time as two Calaveras County sheriff's cruisers that are also pulling up to a remote house on the edge of the forest. The detective and deputies make their way over a swaying wooden footbridge. Stepping off, they wander past a canopy of maple trees and lush willow branches hanging over the pebbles along the creek. The woods grow thick with digger pines and manzanita. Crabtree and the deputies stop at a silver blanket of fallen pine needles under a roof of treetops spread open to the sky's blinding light. One colossal pine tree rises through the center of the glen like an ancient obelisk. A few feet from its base lie the remains of Alex Anderson.

In the coming weeks, the Calaveras County Coroner's Office will officially attribute Alex's death to a massive methamphetamine overdose; and Crabtree will continue to investigate rumors floating through West Point that the boy was murdered with an intentionally lethal dose of meth—a so-called "hot shot"—as a possible way of eliminating risks that came from an amateur addict tampering with a mountain drug world that was more dangerous than he ever had the ability to grasp.

CHAPTER 10
Walking Out of the Shadow

THE KID WATCHED sunlight scorching thistle and edging on pastures and power lines in the dry, brown distance. Handcuffs sped down on his lower arms, cold metal sidewinders that hissed with moving pins, until the bites sunk into a meatless flesh that clung to what remained of his ulnas. Summer rays flashed on the steel. The Kid's limbs brightened a moment. An infected drizzle was clamming around the small needle ulcer in his left elbow. If he had been a real kid—biologically—there might have been a semblance of fear in his eyes, or around the dotted pulp of his nasal tissue. But outwardly and inwardly, The Kid's true age is lost in a skeleton sheathed in worn, mummified skin. He felt a gust run through his long hair, betraying his pupils, wispy mustache growth and a preternatural sweat cooking in the pits of his face. His eyes turned west into the sun, toward the horns of Mount Diablo, a grey altar set over the Delta's depressed fields and waterways. There was little apprehension in his features as they hardened in the evening light. This was not the first time The Kid had been arrested. Maybe, he thought, handcuffs were in his DNA. Growing up, his father was a "prope dope" meth cook for outlaw bikers who rode across California's Bay Area, the region where America's modern methamphetamine nightmare began in the 1960s.

And so The Kid was raised around sliding lines of head dust. He's been in jail cells because of meth. He's waited in clinics because of meth. More relevant to the tremor in his nerve endings, he's witnessed a murder because of meth. A friend's skullcap broken open by a 12-gauge shotgun was the central image that pushed The Kid from snorting crank to shooting it with a needle. The hollow contours of his face still deaden when he thinks of the blood sloshed on his trailer's floor. The killer left. The Kid waited with the body. He lived with it for days before the authorities arrived. After that, there was no place left for him to go but the needle. Sometimes The Kid still plans ways to escape from the cloudy clutch he puts in his arms. No such liberation was planned for the evening when his gaze drifted into the dusk on East Cypress Road, toward the lanes connecting Oakley to a small, river-bound hump of land called Bethel Island. The Kid had nothing more in mind than cruising the seven miles from the island to Oakley's bar. He should have made it—but he wasn't counting on meeting up with Cap.

Captain Lance Morrison of the Newark Police Department is now, after vacating a brief retirement, Officer Lance "Cap" Morrison of the Oakley Police Department. The expertise that sparked Morrison into teaching classes on methamphetamine to law enforcement all over the United States is now applied to watching the homes and harbors along California's central Delta. It's been a good fit for Oakley P.D.'s night shift, which has plenty of use for a drug evaluation expert, especially around Bethel Island, or, as residents of Oakley refer to it, "Methel Island."

The 3,400-acre stretch of soil called Bethel Island, which is tucked in long, deep river channels, has had many lives over the years. Corn, alfalfa and grains flourished throughout the region in the decades leading up to World War II. By the 1950s, an exploding middle class affluent enough to afford boats and ranches poured onto the island's shores to create "an angler's paradise." Vacationers chased large-mouth bass and stripers through Frank's Tract while Black Angus roamed the island's dozens of cattle operations like The Rancho Alena. Today, hints of the lauded resort era are still visible at sunset, when a shimmering rail of light dances down on the slough under the palm trees, reflecting on jeweled stalks of tule, fanning under a humped bridge and down the marina to the pilot house of a gin-joint-era riverboat that's home to the island's Yacht Club.

But a passing tourist doesn't see the reality. To the outside, Bethel Island is another clutter of raised, harbor-side houses, groves of knotted eucalyptus, boats set on calm waters. It still has expensive properties. Little docks remain hidden in the north shore's rambling grass. Its central pastures are dotted with cattle and horses. But, once dark, the bridge lights glint over rusty, stained houseboats tied along Dutch Slough Road. A dimmer illumination hangs east over the run-down trailers with dirty garbage bags fixed on their windows and dismantled car parts strewn across their yards. This is the other face of the angler's paradise, a reality the Delta's methamphetamine addicts simply refer to as "the island." Since transferring to the Oakley Police Department in 2006, Morrison has learned that this world feeds off the boaters—burglarizing yachts on the slough, stealing parts off marine engines, breaking into the few struggling businesses still open. In 2009, Morrison alone made 212

DUI arrests between Oakley and Bethel Island. Nearly half were drunk; but the remaining suspects were all later convicted of driving under the influence of methamphetamine. That same year, a woman fixing the motor to a houseboat on the marina was attacked by a group of female meth addicts. The victim had been kneeling over the gears when her assailants, convinced she had already been paid for the job, rushed her. They beat her with a metal pipe until she was unconscious. They robbed her and then rolled her limp body into the delta waters. Rescued by a fisherman miles down the river, the woman somehow managed to survive. Some officers at Oakley P.D. referred to her as the miracle woman. The Kid didn't like what happened to the woman; but he's stoic enough when it comes to the type of brutality that was dealt at Bethel Island's marina that day. "That's life on the Island," is how he explains it. "The Island is what the Island is. It's its own world. It makes its own rules. It handles things its own way."

With his typical staid demeanor, Morrison arrested The Kid for driving under the influence of a controlled substance. The glare of East Cypress Road filled the patrol car's windows as Cap, turning to his passenger seat, commented to a reporter that places like "the Island" are not supposed to exist anymore. And yet, as evidenced by the scaly, rawboned man hunched in the backseat, they exist all the same. The Federal Combat Methamphetamine Epidemic Act of 2005 was launched to nullify meth's impact by eradicating the countless "mom-and-pop" labs run out of mountain garages and country bathrooms. While that mission was partly successful, the U.S. Department of Justice estimates today that 80 percent of meth in America is either shipped from Mexico, or cooked in new domestic meth labs that are owned, operated and supplied by its drug cartels. The federal government's victory—which was largely environmental—appears to be evaporating by the day. The presence of the cartel-influenced labs can be distinctly felt by those living along the California Delta. On May 12, 2011, Brentwood and Tracy police raided an asparagus farm along Grant Line Canal in the south Delta, netting handguns, rifles, assault weapons and nearly 2 pounds of high-grade crystal methamphetamine packaged for sale. Three men and a woman with probable links to a Mexican drug cartel were arrested on charges ranging from dealing meth to child endangerment. Their operation was located just two miles from where state workers picked a propane tank filled with anhydrous ammonia out of the water near several children who were fishing. From Bethel Island to Rio Vista, these poisonous propane tanks have been known to float into the pockets of swampy bark swill and along the sterns of ships anchored in local harbors.

The Kid is hardly a fan of the state's new meth paradigm: He recalls, with genuine nostalgia, the days when his father could enjoy the power and prestige of being the top cook on a stretch of highway. The Kid knows he will never be able to follow in his old man's footsteps. It is a different world now and whether it's a better world is not a question limited to The Kid and his circle of addicts on Bethel Island. In 2008, the Southern Rural Sociological Association released a major study by Dr. Ralph Weisheit about the ever-changing impact of methamphetamine on the United States. Weisheit, a professor of Criminal Justice at Illinois State University, argued that legal bans on the chemical precursors used for cooking methamphetamine had unforeseen results. "The concern is that the small-scale operators, who mainly cooked for themselves and for friends and for whom small amounts of cash changed hands, are being replaced by large-scale operations in which profit is the driving motive, the money involved is substantial, and the potential for violence is considerable," Weisheit wrote. "Mom-and-pop laboratory operations primarily shared their product with family and friends, and while such operations may have allowed young people access to methamphetamine, there were no strong financial incentives for aggressively marketing their product to youth. In contrast, when methamphetamine production becomes a business run by people with no stake in the well-being of the local community, there are strong incentives for expanding the customer base. The young are a particularly appealing target in that they have the potential to be customers for years."

Weisheit added, "If precursor regulation has had an unclear effect on overall levels of methamphetamine consumption, the effects of these regulations on production patterns seem more clear. Various efforts to regulate methamphetamine production through restrictions on precursors have had the unintended consequence of centralizing production and enriching powerful drug trafficking organizations. It seems likely that an increasingly centralized production and distribution system will also increasingly be associated with violence to protect the enormous profits involved."

In many ways, failures associated with the Federal Combat Methamphetamine Epidemic Act of 2005 signify a broader and well-documented trajectory of miscalculations in the political history around meth. The pattern was established in 1980 when government officials attempted to end the scourge by outlawing propanone, only to encourage a new, more cost-effective version of white powder cooked with ephedrine, an ingredient that is deeply embedded in American life. If the 1980 crackdown on propanone yielded a more socially lethal version of methamphetamine, the 2005 ephedrine lockdown gave drug cartels a stake in rural communities, where traditionally they had none outside of marijuana grows on remote public lands. The marketing structure involved with these groups has spilled blood across the streets of urban America since the 1980s, and continues to do so. The cartels are now arriving in rural America on a road that was arguably paved by the federal government's good intentions. By 2011, politicians in southern states—who were paying little attention to this history—began calling for ephedrine to be entirely banned from the consumer markets. The stance gained popularity with some legislators, despite all indications from national, state and local law enforcement agencies across the country that such measures, while gravely punishing legitimate cold and sinus sufferers, would have very little effect on the overall supply of methamphetamine to addicts.

After nearly thirty years of battling meth on the same California streets that gave birth to the modern Frankenstein, Lance Morrison is convinced that new laws and regulations are, at best, Band-Aids. To look at The Kid, or to look at the shabby houseboats of the central Delta, all one needs to know is that wherever the cultural hunger exists, methamphetamine keeps going and going.

IN MAY 1997, Dr. Michael Sise, a trauma surgeon, appeared at The National Methamphetamine Drug Conference in Omaha, Nebraska, cautioning fellow experts that methamphetamine addiction was a diagnosis worse than cancer. "You will inevitably die," Sise told the gathering, "whether directly or indirectly, from the use of methamphetamine." Citing extreme treatment difficulties, Sise went on to advocate for strong prevention programs for first-time use. The challenges Sise was alluding to involve the incredible failure rates of methamphetamine addicts trying to stay clean. By 2011, some national experts estimated meth's overall relapse rate was as high as 92 percent. Meaningful statistics around criminal recidivism for addicts pulled back into their addiction are difficult to come by; though a probation probe that was conducted in Amador County, California, in 2009—which found that 50 percent of all felony offenders being monitored in the county had a known history of methamphetamine use—suggests that the numbers are likely high.

Despite daunting figures around methamphetamine, some rural communities are experiencing hope in prevention campaigns like The Montana Meth Project. Dr. Sise had stressed the need for such programs back in 1997; though it was not until eight years later, when philanthropist Tom Siebel stepped forward to organize and help pay for it, that a real movement began to take hold. The statistical victories the MMP gained for its state between 2005 and 2011 resulted from a combination of research-based messaging, public-private coalitions and a relentless barrage of "shock ads" aimed at Montana's youth. While the shock ads have been controversial, a passing glance at American culture may offer a clue as to why the tactic is so effective. Teenagers in even the most isolated rural counties do not exist in a vacuum from popular entertainment. Where televisions and the Internet are present, young viewers and users see the immense value mainstream media places on personal appearance. They sense the way it promotes codified vanity. They feel its bombardment of unapologetic celebrity worship, which, in the end, circles back to the nation's obsession with image. By raising billboards on highways adorned with toothless mouths and blister-bombed faces the MMP was tapping a subconscious nerve vital to American youth: The ghost of gradual repulsiveness stresses consequences of meth use to teens in a way their cultural programming cannot reconcile or ignore. Montana's 62-percent drop in teen meth use since the MMP launched suggests the power of the images is inescapable.

Jim Langford and his colleagues at the Georgia Meth Project spent 2009 and 2010 creating a model that was "nearly identical" to the MMP. At the same time, community leaders and proactive businesses also launched The Arizona Meth Project, The Colorado Meth Project, The Hawaii Meth Project, The Idaho Meth Project, The Illinois Meth Project and The Wyoming Meth Project. MMP spokesperson Sarah Ingram confirms that other states have considered linking with the movement. "There's an interest in a lot of other locations," she says. "A place like California could really use one."

Even with reasons to be optimistic about America's youth, the legion of current methamphetamine addicts comprise a social force that has to be rescued or reckoned with. On a span of the Edwards Plateau in west-central Texas, that task falls to the Star Council on Substance Abuse, the main agency offering treatment programs for addicts in seven rural counties between Fort Worth, Waco and Abilene.

The Star Council has offices in locations like the city of Stephenville, population 15,000. Stephenville boasts a continuum of cowboys and muscular Texas longhorns grazing on its fields and ridges. On East Washington Street, pickup trucks roll into the largest private country and western club in the largest state in the lower 48. On Saturday nights, residents of all ages attend family music shows at the neon-lit Cross Timbers Country Opry. Just down Highway 377, Lone Star Arena is proof that Stephenville's famed rodeo tradition is still bucking strong. Rodeos in the area have even been used to raise funds for members of the community, as in the case of Eliva Rodriguez, who looked on as roughnecks wrestled steers and team-roped calves in an effort to help with medical costs she was facing after being diagnosed with stage 4 stomach cancer. Scenes from Stephenville are arguably the very image of the western United States; however, the fight to stop methamphetamine from eating away at the lives of some residents has been a hard one, partly due to the same factors that give the area its character and charm.

Cassandra Hanna has been a treatment specialist for the Star Council for six years. Before coming to the ranches of Erath County, she worked in Amarillo. She quickly learned that rural communities face major challenges in battling addiction. "The towns I'm working in now are generally underserved when it comes to getting financial support to deal with the problems they're facing," Hanna says. "It seems like a majority of funding gets sent to the big metropolitan areas, so there's a basic lack of resources, from clinics to mental health services to transportation. In fact, out here, the lack of transportation is one of the biggest issues that comes up: We have clients who have to drive more than twenty miles to get to their treatment program. Some don't have vehicles. Others have lost their license. They still have to try to find rides here several times a week. The clients who do have cars have to deal with soaring gas prices they can't always afford. It's part of life out in the country, but it certainly makes it harder for certain people to get help."

The Star Council relies heavily on federal block grants and support from the Texas Department of State Health Services to provide treatment. A number of the areas it works in, such as Comanche County and Eastland County, have roughly 17 percent of the population living below the poverty line. Grant funding allows Star to provide services, based on a sliding scale of income, for men and women diagnosed with substance abuse dependency. Most treatment programs run sixteen to twenty weeks. Individuals with health insurance or Medicaid can voluntarily commit themselves at any of Star's clinics for help, but it's encounters with the Texas criminal justice system or the Texas child protective services that account for the vast majority of referrals to the organization. Hanna believes part of that phenomenon can be attributed to the stigma around illegal drug addiction that exists in places like Stephenville, which has been ranked among "The Best 100 small towns in America."

"We still haven't convinced all of these rural communities that we really have drug problems," Hanna observes. "Methamphetamine is what we see the most of; but we have serious issues with alcoholism and illegal prescription drugs. When you live in a small town where it feels like no one is talking about addiction, it creates an atmosphere that makes people seeking treatment worry a lot about being judged. Here in Stephenville, our office is basically across the street from the police station. A good number of clients are worried about being seen coming in, because they know people will talk."

The addicts who do come to the Star Council for help face a host of challenges. Specialists like Hanna work to teach clients to develop a multi-problem focus when tackling their addictions — a holistic view of every obstacle and condition of life that is hindering the addict from staying clean. The counselors stress the importance of an addict being able to identify their own patterns of behavior, particularly the physical and emotional triggers that cause relapse. The addicts are also encouraged to find a dependable support network. The treatment is constant work. It takes unfailing dedication. It requires excruciating vulnerability. For those hooked on methamphetamine, it is often the most difficult ordeal the addict's ever confronted.

"We tell our clients that they have to be fully committed to their own treatment," Hanna says, referencing the fact that many clients have come to Star Council in lieu of jail or prison time. "If they're not truly committed, then it doesn't really matter what their counselors do, they won't have meaningful progress. We do have a lot of individuals who are coming in because the criminal justice system has said they have to. Usually, once we get them in, we try to do some effective motivational interviewing up front. We try to help them uncover what their own reasons really are for wanting to work on their addiction. It's a lot of work; but I think in most cases, after the client has been through the entire program, they understand that they needed help and that it's up to them to make the most of that help."

MATTHEW LEARNED no longer waits for the shadow people. He used to be ready for them during those dark nights when he would stand outside his trailer with a loaded 9mm in hand, his skull cooking with the image of silhouettes that moved through the rock quarry on the edge of the city. He could sense them summoning across the wisteria glow on the pastures. He could almost feel them sneaking and scurrying through the hot sweat on his forehead.

Clean from methamphetamine for seven years now, Matthew Learned no longer waits for the shadow people. But real people can be frightening enough to a man who's come out of Pelican Bay Prison, considered the most dangerous correctional facility in all of California. In a quiet corner of El Dorado County, Matt spends his afternoons helping his parents with landscaping and yard work. He pushes a wheelbarrow along, meditating on books he's borrowed from the library. He knocks the rolling perspiration from his brow, longing to spend more time with the daughter he's still getting to know. Matthew John Learned. His Christian name could hardly invoke more irony—for Matt *has* learned. He's learned what the cost is for being branded with fifty-five arrest incidents and four servings of hard prison time. He's learned about his problems with concentration after subjecting his brain to thirty years of chemical heating and cooling. When recollections manage to break through the skipping in his glial cells, images rushing back literally nauseate him. Above all, Matt has learned that coming back to the world at age 50 means having the courage to own what he's done, acknowledge who he's been and will himself to be someone better. Only Matthew Learned can kill the old Matthew Learned.

Matt's life never had to take this path. He is the first to admit it. His parents were honest and hardworking. He grew up in a safe neighborhood in California's cutting-edge Silicon Valley. He went to the same junior high school as Apple Computer co-founder Steve Jobs—whom he knew—and attended Monta Vista, ranked among the top high schools in the United States by *Newsweek* and the *Washington Post*. Matt was getting good grades. He was in the process of joining a high-paying union.

"I had every opportunity I ever could have asked for," Matt now admits. "It was the all-American upbringing. And there's no other way to say it: I just threw it all away."

For Matt, the hurricane started turning with the sheer force of the 1980s. The decade moved through his senses in a reckless blur of marijuana bowls and lines of cocaine humped on dirty mirrors. His world changed in 1989 when he first smoked methamphetamine. Matt's high had evolved into a train of stimulation with the first stop a prison in Tamal. He had been convicted of felony hit-and-run in his Nissan 280 ZX. The charge alleged he had caused gross bodily injury to a victim while driving under the influence of alcohol and methamphetamine. Four years later, Matt exited prison and headed for a backwoods puddle of the Gold Country in north El Dorado. He was on meth again. He was spending his time with a circle of addicts committing thefts and burglaries in houses along the steep canyons. Matt was not even free a year before the El Dorado County Sheriff's Office put him in handcuffs again. Convicted of receiving known stolen property, he spent another twelve months in a state penitentiary.

Matt walked out into freedom in 1997. Rather than go back to El Dorado County, he opted for neighboring Amador County. He was soon holed up in a trailer park in Ione—a tin, hyperactive world of yards crowded with broken chairs, landscapes of withered bull thistle, flammable empty lots, a spidery, leaf-blown van that hadn't moved in a decade. Matt had stumbled on a makeshift addict's paradise. The tweakers thrived after sundown. They wiped raw nose blisters and listened for messages on their CB radios. "I just saw Bill on the hill," truckers would say into their mics after 11 p.m., as their eighteen-wheelers rolled on Highway 88. "I've got a load on the road." It was the signal between big rig drivers and late night addicts that ran on two channels—a coded confirmation that there was methamphetamine to buy off the truck. Other signals from the rigs were more obvious. Matt would hear the truckers clicking hard on their CBs to announce, "Hey, hey, you've got a tweaker in your speaker!" Occasionally, when a driver had a really fresh bag of meth, he would steam through Ione, keying up his mic in rapid fire, huffing, "Audio! Audio! Audio check!"

In the darkest hours of the morning, Matt could hear the spinners blathering to each other from corners of the park. He could hear their crystal-smoked sex serenades. He listened to addicts turning violent at random moments, tearing their trailers to pieces. "Practically everybody in the park was on meth back then," Matt remembers. "Your so-called friends would be tweaking for days, and they'd break into your place and steal your things, and turn around and try to sell it to your other 'friends.' It was a cutthroat world; but you got used to it, because your head's not in reality. You saw everything through a meth prism, and you just thought that it was the way things were."

The more methamphetamine Matt used, the more his behavior adapted to the paranoid mode of life in the park. He tinted his trailer windows and hooked a 12-volt radar detector to one of their frames, scanning for police cars. He concealed microphones along his walkway with wires running into speakers in his bedroom, so he could hear any footsteps approach. His most inventive maneuver was mixing half-a-gram of meth with water in a spray bottle, and then spraying a mist over the floor of his entire trailer, hoping to torment any drug-sniffing

K-9s brought in during a raid. Sometimes Matt would snort a long line of meth and spend hours hosing down his driveway in the middle of the night, pressure-blasting every single inch of it, over and over.

Matt eventually became so entwined in the blinds-bending nervousness of the park that he began to consider himself its sheriff. That meant carrying a loaded 9mm in his right pocket and having a sweeper shotgun—12 gauge, 12 rounds—ready to grab at any moment in his bedroom. As a convicted felon, Matt was taking a risk of earning "strike-able" offenses under California law, three of which could send him to prison for life. He felt no fear; not even as a new name started getting whispered around the trailer park: Amador County Sheriff's Detective Jim Wegner. To the addicts, he was "King of the 5-0," a narcotics agent with the frame of a football linebacker and a tenacity that swung the biggest proverbial boot in the Mother Lode. Matt and Wegner were on their own collision course that very year. It was 8 a.m when Wegner kicked open the door of Matt's trailer. His target had been on a meth-powered homerun that blocked sleep for one-hundred-and-forty hours and running. Matt had just dropped down on his couch. He was in the act of finally passing out, eyes fluttering shut—when the concussive crash of the doorknob against the wall rammed through his consciousness. Deputies in masks fanned into his trailer with their guns drawn.

Matt spent another year in state prison for possession of methamphetamine. He knew that as soon as he was released he would be back in the wide-eyed thiefdom of his trailer park. And the felon returned to Ione with his sights set on elevating his position in the meth game. Matt anointed himself a crank cook of the open west county. Lording over a meth supply, he was fooling enough addicts to boost his prestige, but he was not fooling himself. The operation required saving money for ingredients and precursors; Matt lived fast and spent faster. His haste also led to minor disasters while cooking his meth. The process took patience. More than half of the batches concocted in the new chef's trailer were useless. Matt never worried about basking in acids and chemical compounds. Any fear of burning to death in his trailer, or snuffing an innocent neighbor in an explosion, was absent from his mind. He had once had a code, which included giving no respect to meth cooks who put sanitation workers at risk, or poured toxins down drains, leaching poisons into the county's soil and ground water supplies. But he was now hovering, in his own words, in a dream-like "insanity" where afternoons and evenings merged into a bleared theater of compulsion.

Wegner's narcotics detectives were watching the trailer park. In 2004, they finally eliminated the name Matthew Learned from their to-do list for good. Time had stood still that day. Matt was holding a pipe to his lips, clenching his chest and "gassing his dope" when he heard voices outside shouting to his neighbors. "Stay inside," one of the men commanded, "Get back in your house." Matt jumped up to look out his back window. He was staring into the lampblack barrels of two assault rifles.

Locked in county jail, Matt was soon caught by Wegner lying to his own father about meth residue being dusted over some Learned family belongings confiscated during the raid. Wegner had had enough. He sent a message to Matt: "You need to stop lying, get real and man up." Slumped in a holding cell, the words gradually penetrated Matt's bruised, throbbing skull. A psychic mirror lifted into his thoughts, turning with reflections of humiliation and ugliness the addict could scarcely comprehend.

"I don't know why, but for some reason those words woke me up and made me see myself in different way," Matt remembers. "They made me see Wegner in a different way, too. It was just one sentence, but it hit me like a bomb."

Wegner's voice was still echoing in Matt's memories the day he was brought for sentencing before Amador County Superior Court Judge David Richmond. Richmond was proud to be a small-county judge, and known for trying to use fairness and respect as guiding principles to weigh out justice. The judge was also known for being sincerely encouraging to drug addicts who were trying to get clean. In an attempt to avoid going back to prison, Matt petitioned the court to defer his prison sentence to the Delancy Street treatment program in San Francisco.

"I wish I could send you there, Mr. Learned," Richmond said in a concerned voice. "In this case, the law doesn't allow it. But if I could do that, I would."

Richmond's demeanor kept Matt's spirits up as the bailiffs led him off. It was the judge's unrushed engagement, the long, direct eye contact, the honed attentiveness in his face. "It was just another one of those moments that helped the light come on," Matt recalls. "I could see that I was an actual person to the judge, and that he really wanted to help me. That's when I started to get it—I finally understood there were people who cared more about me than I cared about myself."

Matt was transported to Pelican Bay Prison to brave a four-year sentence. He started the first twenty-four hours of it with a basic promise to himself to steer clear of smuggled methamphetamine. He began working as an aide in the prison's Level

1 Medical Center. Matt quickly got the staff's attention with his organizational skills. He impressed them with his consistent dependability. Soon, he was being treated like a valued member of their team. It was the first time in three decades Matt felt needed by people outside of the meth world—a world he increasingly viewed as constructed of lies, manipulation and mutual abuse. Matt had a new drive to become the best hospital aide the staff had ever worked with. In time, he was promoted to an unofficial office manager for the center. Legitimate pride in legitimate work: It was all part of continuing to wake from the long, labored dream. News came that Matt had a daughter born on the outside. Family members eventually sent him a photograph of the toddler on a rocking horse with her little hands reaching for the sky. Matt laughed at her pose, thinking of Wegner and his deputies. As the days rolled on Matt's main wish was to meet his daughter. He wanted to learn to be a real father. He wanted to know what it was to have a meaningful purpose. For the moment, all he could do was focus on the clinic, seeing it as training to hold down a full-time job on the path to becoming a responsible father.

In March of 2008, Matt walked out of Pelican Bay holding a stack of recommendation letters from doctors and nurses who had come to genuinely value his talents and his attitude. He began working with counselors to help him understand the nature of the addiction that had stolen so many years of his life. Matt knew he needed a game plan to protect him from his past. He cut off all ties with the meth addicts he had known in the hills, choosing to live in self-imposed exile with his parents on the southern outskirts of El Dorado County. He got a library card and began ingesting books on psychology, parenting and early childhood development. He reestablished a connection with his family, helping his mom and dad with projects around the house. Most importantly to Matt, he began having visitations with his daughter.

Outsiders to addiction might have guessed Matt was making a seamless transition back into society. He was staying clean from methamphetamine; but the journey was fraught with confusion. The longer it went on, the more he felt a spear of loneliness running through him on a daily basis. "When I was on meth, I felt invincible," is how he explains it. "I was the man. I thought there was no one smarter than me. I thought there was no one tougher than me. When sobriety truly sets in, and you're living in the real world, you feel like you're nobody. There's this sense that you're the most insignificant person alive. You have to learn to exist that way, and hope things will be better."

For Matt, his daughter's face was the barometer that kept him hoping. He framed his picture of her on the rocking horse, overlapped by his prison booking photo—Learned, M: H-79208—as well as his official release card from the California Department of Corrections. The items represented Matt's past, present and future, with the largest image proof that being a father was the only thing he had ever been proud of in his life. That pride helped keep him calm in 2009, when his parole ended. It was the most frightening day he had ever experienced. The training wheels were off. The state of California had wiped its hands of him. The new Matthew Learned—sober, stoic and unemployed—was left alone with himself. He continued getting counseling. He also went back to dwelling on a voice that had stayed with him during his entire stint in prison: *Stop lying, get real and man up.* The deep, slow roll of Detective Wegner's voice was as vivid in his mind as ever. Scanning newspaper articles, Matt found that Wegner had been promoted to second-in-command of the Amador County Sheriff's Office.

Matt felt a strong desire to contact the man who had sent him to Pelican Bay. He phoned the sheriff's office and asked for Wegner. To his surprise, within a few seconds of speaking to the receptionist, that unmistakable voice came on the line. "This is Matthew Learned," the nervous ex-con said.

The phone connection was slightly muffled. Wegner wasn't sure if he was talking to Matthew Learned or Matthew David. "Ok," the Undersheriff replied. "Which Matt? The one from Pine Grove, or the one from Ione?"

"Ione."

"How can I help you?"

"I wanted to say something to you," Matt commented in a neutral tone.

Unshakable, Wegner kept the receiver to his ear. "Lay it on me."

"Thank you," Matt said. "What you said really had an impact on my life. It took a few years, but I realized I had to stop lying and man up; because I wasn't lying to anyone but myself. You know, my life was all about meth and the trash that came with it … I never wanted to be hooked on meth, but I was, and meth causes you to think that there's no life without it."

Matt went on to mention that he had real problems in his new life, but he was determined to face them without using. Wegner was supportive, and told Matt that the arrests were never personal.

Matt also made a phone call to Amador County Superior Court Judge David Richmond, thanking him for treating him like a human at a time he wasn't sure he was one. In the coming months Matt agreed to be interviewed for a newspaper article about the connection between crime and methamphetamine. He had spent more than thirty years watching his fellow meth addicts engage in burglaries, auto theft, check fraud, larcenies and other felony acts, and he was more than willing to share those memories with the public. He also weighed in on the effectiveness of California's controversial law, Proposition 36, which is billed as a common sense way of getting non-violent drug offenders court-supervised treatment rather than prison time. Asked about Proposition 36's numerous and noted failures—including instances where it had allowed addicts who would have been incarcerated to progress to wider burglary sprees and cases of child abuse—Matt replied that the issue of weighing court-ordered treatment against protecting the public is riddled with challenges. "If an addict gets into the habit of stealing, they're going to keep going at it until they're clean," he told the reporter. "Once you get off the drugs, you look back at what you've done and it's just sickening. But you have to have that clarity, first." He added, "Court-ordered treatment can work, if the person really wants it. The problem is that, a lot of times, addicts simply choose the program because it's a much easier ride than jail time or prison. If they're committing crimes, they can keep doing it. I think a person should only get it if they can really explain to the judge why they want to better themselves. If they can't, then they're just another person playing the system—and those are the addicts who ruin it for everyone."

Matt did not ask the newspaper to change or obscure his name, nor did he ask the reporter to downplay the amount of time he had spent in prison. If he wanted his life to be taken seriously as a cautionary tale, he'd decided, then it would have to be clear that the endless string of arrests, jail stints and prison terms had been real—and were all part of the real man, Matthew Learned, who had been on methamphetamine. And his childhood seemed more important than ever now. Good parents. A safe neighborhood. An excellent school. He knew what stereotypes the public has of meth addicts. He had fully embodied the grotesque image at one time; but not in the beginning. In the beginning he had possessed every advantage.

Now that Matt Learned no longer waits for the shadow people at night, that's the meaning he finds in his own story.

"I'd be willing to sit down with anyone and show them the house I grew up in, or my grades and all of the great things that have been written about the high school I attended," Matt says, "because that is who I was; but, in the next breath, I'd have to show them my rap sheet, the fact that I've been arrested fifty-five times, that I've been discharged from Pelican Bay. Because that's me, too; and there's no point in running from it. When I look at everything I had going for me when I was young, it's pretty clear that if getting pulled into meth addiction could happen to me, it could happen to anyone. And that's a hard thing to know. I just shake my head looking back at how I wasted my life. I was the devil—the devil had me."

EPILOGUE

Ione, California: April 13

IT'S 11:43 P.M. The ex-convict steers his Ford toward the gas station, studying a gnat-peppered, apricot glow cast on weathered signs and the knotted forms of tree torsos. He glances in his rearview mirror to see an Ione Police cruiser rolling onto Preston Avenue, steadily moving in. Cat and mouse. The ex-con, 47-year-old Kevin Otterbein, measures the predatory pace of the cruiser's running lights. They are coming fast, so Otterbein suddenly decides to hit his turn signal and pull between the dusty pumps of the Chevron station. He watches the black-and-white swoop by.

Two minutes pass before Otterbein brings his Ford back onto the avenue. He turns for the ranchlands of Highway 124 under a moon throwing azure-steel on rows of passing clouds. Beyond, thin spines of stock fence lift from wild grass, and the Ford's lights push down the open route to Plymouth, which Otterbein knows will return him safely to the distant mountains. The ex-convict is sure his gas station-evasion trick worked. It's a maneuver most dealers carry in their repertoires, predictable, but effective.

A manic flurry of red-and-blue radiance punches through

the Ford's cab. Otterbein can sense it clicking around him, filling the seats, sweeping past to the steer and the high fans of sage in the outer darkness. He brings the truck to a stop. The ex-con doesn't know the man following him since Preston Avenue is Ione police officer Josh Long. It would have been good information to have; because the addicts of Matthew Learned's old trailer park could have told Otterbein that the game was over before it started.

Crime and addiction have continued to thrive in the trailer park since the day Matt Learned was hauled off for his appointment with Pelican Bay Prison. To the local meth culture, the Amador County Sheriff's Office remains a constant fear factor on the open ranch roads beyond the city; however, in 2007, the six-officer force that comprises the Ione Police Department quickly became an equal threat after chief Michael Johnson was hired under the promise of creating a new, fully-professional department that would hit the city's meth problem by relentlessly targeting dealers. Johnson brought three new recruits into the department, and one was Josh Long, fresh out of the police academy and poised to have rookie and sophomore years that drug traffickers wouldn't soon forget. Vehicle search after vehicle search, Long and his partner, Officer Jason Peppas, found bags of methamphetamine. The white, wrapped prizes were often accompanied by stolen property and illegal weapons. Dealers began to realize there was no use hiding a stash when the Ione police lights came on. By 2011, Peppas had been promoted to a narcotics detective. He was replaced as Long's partner by a sleek, black 78-pound German Sheppard named Pras. Long's arrest numbers, particularly with methamphetamine, continued to climb.

You're a young meth dealer standing on the corner of East Jackson Street and Arroyo Street, product in your pocket and a pellet gun just to look dangerous, and here comes Long walking straight at you. He throws you and your "gangster" friends into the back of his patrol car before one meaningful transaction can go down. It's midnight. You're pulled over on a lightless corner of Main Street giving Long consent to search your vehicle, because no one hides methamphetamine inside a beater-on-wheels like you. But then your throat seizes as the officer tugs on the loose ignition switch, carefully prying it from the steering column to tease your crank stash out like a dirty, distorted string of pearls. Or, you're a veteran meth dealer, a certified pro at hauling ashen crystal from Stockton into the southwestern Gold Country, where addicts are terrified by rumors you're a hit man for the Hells Angels—and now Long is tossing your truck, pulling the evidence together for a felony transportation case that could get you eight years in state prison.

Long's reputation began to do some of the work for him. He arrested one young probationer for walking through Ione with a pocket full of meth. A week later, after the suspect posted bail, Long noticed him sauntering down an avenue and decided to check on him. One glimpse of Long and the probationer immediately stopped on his own, put his hands over his head and spread his legs, calling over his shoulder: "Right, back pocket."

Long hesitated. "What's in you're right back pocket?"

"Same as last time," the young man responded. "Only more."

On a warm summer evening Long stopped his patrol car to talk to a meth user who was wandering into Matthew Learned's old trailer park. "Hey, I know you," Long observed as he got out.

"I know you, too," the addict shot back, nervously. "Everybody out here knows who the fuck you are."

When the local newspaper ran its fifteenth story about one of Long's methamphetamine arrests, a radio personality wryly observed, "If I was a drug dealer, I think I would stay as far away as I could from the city of Ione." Meanwhile, a few cops and reporters were beginning to refer to Long as "the Tweeker Hammer," or, simply, "The Hammer."

But all of this history is unknown to Kevin Otterbein, a convict who's been on a recent meth slide in the northeastern mountains of Amador County. Otterbein only knows that the gas station-evasion routine has failed him; and that a tall, broad-shouldered officer is making his way to the driver's window. Otterbein slowly rolls his window down.

"Evening," Long says. "The reason I pulled you over" — but the young officer's eyes are already following his flashlight through the truck cab, slightly ahead of his thought process but not ahead of his instincts, which warn that something is out of place. Long sweeps his light over the passenger seat, slowing on a bag of hypodermic needles in plain view next to a large knife with a swastika on its handle. He brings the flashlight closer to the driver's face: Two wide-blown pupils shutter back at him. A visible sweat is clamming around Otterbein's biker bandana, trembling out his pores to roll down two large, crossing scars that form a jagged X on his forehead.

"Do you have a medical need for those needles?" Long asks.

"What?"

"Do you have diabetes?"

"No."

"What are the needles for?"

"What?"

"I need you to step out of the vehicle for a minute."

"Why?"

"Just step out for a minute."

Otterbein dumps his boots down onto a pool of gravel, stretching inside his heavy army jacket. Long directs him to turn around.

"Fuck this," the suspect blurts, rearing up with resistance; but the handcuffs are already fastening.

"Relax," Long tells him in a calm voice. "I need to pat you down. Do you have any weapons?"

"No."

"Any blades or needles that are going to poke me?"

"No."

Long moves a gloved hand up Otterbein's chest and hits a stun gun that's fastened inside a shoulder strap. "Well," he quips, "that would have been nice to know about."

Otterbein is positioned on the hood of the patrol car. Long begins a search of the Ford, moving clothes around the needles to find a chunk of crystal methamphetamine the size of his cell phone—an 8-gram rock—next to another bag of meth, a bag of cocaine and a plethora of illegal pills.

The Hammer has struck again.

Yet it's not until Long has a chance to conduct a full search, and track Otterbein's criminal history, that he begins to understand the gravity of those first seconds when he walked up to the Ford's window. Kevin Otterbein has done four stints in Folsom Prison. When Long pulled him over, he was legally one "strike" away from spending the rest of his life behind bars. Behind the seat of the Ford, Long discovers a loaded 9mm pistol with a round in the chamber, ready to fire, where Otterbein could have grabbed it during the stop. He also finds a loaded .22-caliber pistol, with a round in the chamber, ready to fire, hidden on the passenger seat under a dirty rag—even easier to grab than the 9mm. Knives are concealed around the cab. A blackjack is lying near the tailgate. Towards the end of the search, Long finds a baton tucked under a sleeping bag. "What's this?" he calls over to Otterbein. Before the ex-con can answer, Long touches a small button and watches the stick break into two long swords that gleam in each of his hands. "What the…"

"That's just something I found," Otterbein shouts back. His words cut over the sound of his cell phone erupting on the hood of the patrol car. Long realizes the suspect's phone is lit with the fifteenth incoming call since the traffic stop began. In each case, the name flashing on the caller I.D. reads "Hillbilly."

"Guess someone really wants to know where you are," Long observes. "I must have made you late for an important meeting." The bulging lassoes in Otterbein's eyes stay locked on his phone. He doesn't say a word. Rocking in his handcuffs, sweat bumping on his temples, he stares hard at the name Hillbilly as it flashes over and over again. Long continues searching the trash-filled vehicle. More knives. Methamphetamine residue dusted across the steering console. The moon sails through a pearly screen of clouds and the broken pastures grow dim. No sign of another law enforcement unit. Like many small, incorporated cities, Ione can only afford to have one police officer working after sundown. Backup often comes from the sheriff's office; but tonight whichever deputy is covering the four-hundred-square-mile western county beat is handling a call. And the cell phone keeps ringing. Hillbilly wants answers. Long tells

Otterbein he is under arrest before moving him into the cruiser's backseat. Focusing, Long starts to lay the drugs and weapons across the hood of the car. The cell phone rings again; but this time Hillbilly appears to cut his own transmission off. Long is leaning into the Ford's cab seconds later when he notices two headlights suddenly appear down the corridor of shadows. Even from a distance he can tell it's not a sheriff's unit. The lights roll slow, gradually spanning bigger on the highway, sliding through bent oaks and rough, leaning fences. The Hammer lifts his formidable shoulders up with the driver's door still touching his back. He watches the truck continue to approach. The foreign headlights blaze over his patrol car, illuminating the confiscated guns, bags of methamphetamine and the arsenal of hand weapons. Long sees the brake lights go cherry. Dropping his hand on his gun, the officer starts to push away from the door. The truck slows to a creep. Long's .40 caliber is coming free from its holster when the truck—all at once—accelerates by him, gaining speed on the lightless roadway, until its taillights are finally swallowed by a cool blackness on the open range.

Long walks over to the hood of his cruiser and looks at Otterbein's phone: It's lifeless. It never rings again during the search.

A night wind sweeps through the brome, humming above a guttural choir of bullfrogs just past the scattered live oaks. The highway begins to brighten again. A new set of headlights drives up at a smooth, even pace. Long watches a familiar sedan roll to a stop, and Jackson police detective Chris Rice is already out and heading over before the sound of its engine dies. Rice was on a surveillance assignment when he heard about Long's contact with Otterbein over the radio. The detective knew who

Otterbein was, and he soon understood from the radio silence that no sheriff's deputies or highway patrol officers in the county were free to make it to Long's position. Pausing to glance at the suspect, Rice drops a thumb down onto the gold star on his belt and walks over to Long. His stare shifts across to the neat arrangement of contraband on the cruiser's hood, including the illegal hand weapons and the two loaded guns that had been positioned where Otterbein could grab them during the stop. It is in these quiet moments when officer Andrew Stevens is still very much present in the minds of law enforcement across California: Shot in the face on a routine traffic stop, killed without a chance to react, murdered by a common, low-level criminal who was high on methamphetamine. Rice picks up Otterbein's 9mm, pulling its slide to see the round in the chamber. He sets it down and then picks up the .22 caliber, finding that it has a hot round ready. He lays the second gun down against the steel of the hood, red-and-blue tracers turning rhythmically against a contemplative stare in his pale eyes.

CHRIS RICE SPENT a good deal of 2011 testifying in court proceedings. To half-retired bailiffs and quiet defense attorneys, the common sight of the investigator strolling by in a pressed, tailored suit made it obvious that his caseloads from the previous two years were substantial. By teaming up with agents from the Amador County Sheriff's Office, Amador County District Attorney's Office and California Highway Patrol, Rice took part in 350 investigations, executed 60 search warrants, handled nearly 130 parole and probation searches and was involved with over 390 arrests. During that time, he and his colleagues seized 36 handguns, 37 rifles, 15 shotguns, more than 530 grams of methamphetamine and 1,380 pseudoephedrine pills, still the main ingredient used for cooking meth. These investigations took place in Amador County, California, population 34,000.

Rice never missed a court date. Bits and pieces of the 390 cases rolled on, until the preliminary hearings, the violation of probation dates and the occasional trials began to slide into a numb sense of the routine. By the end 2011, only a few of the meth offenders who weren't guilty of child abuse stood out in Rice's mind, and, when they did, it was usually for a specific reason. There was the serial burglar who had been caught by Jackson police officer Mike Collins with stolen property, a loaded gun and methamphetamine. Despite having already suffered a conviction for elder abuse, the burglar had been given probation, failed it and then been caught by Rice stealing firearms and a stash of gold flakes from another residence. He was in possession of methamphetamine when Rice took him into custody. Sentenced to three years in prison, the man was granted a brief cruise waiver to assist his mother with personal affairs. Rice got a phone call a few days later saying that the man had been found hanging from a barn. Rice also remembers testifying against two suspected methamphetamine dealers from Pioneer in September of 2011. One of the alleged traffickers hired Ken Foley, a trial lawyer who for decades has specialized in handling drug cases. Rice and Detective Justin Colletti, from the Amador County Sheriff's Office, spent the better part of four hours telling a judge about the methamphetamine, packaging materials, crystal meth pipes and hypodermic needles loaded with liquid meth they had found in the couple's apartment, as well as text messages calling for digital scales and asking "who has some shit." After the proceedings ended, Foley walked by the two detectives in front of the courthouse and stopped to holler, "That was the biggest crock of prejudicial bullshit I've ever heard in my life!" The two men stood in silence as they watched Foley stomp off, climb into the passenger seat of an Aladdin Bail bondsman's van and get chauffeured away by its driver.

But most cases don't stand out for Rice as anything more than components to a deeper, institutionalized knowledge of the central Gold Country's drug world. A suspect like Christopher Jarrod Stockton, a.k.a., "the Giant" can be captured and sent back to prison for violation of parole, and it's little more than coffee machine banter at the start of another long surveillance detail. Kevin Otterbein escaped earning his third strike in California, instead opting into a plea bargain that sent him back to state prison for seven years. Some offenders like Justin Solansky, who danced half-naked on methamphetamine in the streets of Ione, never even saw the inside of a courtroom. Solansky simply fled the region after posting bail. These cases are routine. There are a hundred Stocktons, Otterbeins and Solanskys in each corner of the little county these officers watch over.

IN MARCH OF 2011, methamphetamine reared its head in a disturbing encounter for officer Mike Collins. Like many in Jackson, Collins watched as his little city attempted to come back from a state of near death brought on by the Great Recession. New businesses were finally moving into Main Street's eighteen vacant storefronts. The timeless avenue's brickwork was being repainted in cool Victorian hues. Downtown's titanic icon, the National Hotel, was enjoying a 2 million dollar restoration. All around, Jacksonsonians saw cause for optimism. Yet, on that spring afternoon, amidst the busy construction work, a 911 emergency summoned the Jackson Police Department to a bank on Main Street. Collins pulled up. Through the glass he saw a tall man with a damp mop of hair hovering near the tellers and blabbering into a dead cell phone. Three seconds through the door and Collins was catching all the signs of methamphetamine—a lot of methamphetamine—roiling through the man's blood. He was perpetually shaking. His lips jerked up in tight contractions. With eyes that were flame-shot, watery and wide, the man launched into a spun soliloquy about how there was no one in the room he could trust. Collins looked at his pupils, which were dilated to a full 7 mm. The officer attempted to conduct a pat down for weapons, only to see his suspect explode into a paranoid frenzy. "You're a demon!" the man screamed, pulling away from Collins, "You're a demon, I know it—you're a god damn demon."

"What did you take?" Collins demanded.

The unraveling addict admitted to just snorting half a gram of methamphetamine he'd found on the ground. A fight broke out when Collins attempted to control his movements. Jackson city fire captain Frank Tremaine saw Collins struggling and tackled the suspect by his legs. After handcuffs ended the incident, paramedics took the man's vitals: Blood pressure 154/110—heart rate 120 beats per minute. "Right in the middle of the afternoon on Main Street," Collins uttered in disbelief later that evening. "And the guy wasn't even that bad once he started coming down. He told me he needed help, and that he was stupid for having used crank he found on the street."

Meth's presence continues to grind on the shield Collins wears on his chest, just as it does across the river for Calaveras County sheriff's detective Josh Crabtree. The investigator soldiered through the close of 2011 fielding burglaries, rapes and one more meth-related homicide. Through it all, Alex Anderson was never far from his thoughts. Rumors have persisted that the fifteen-year-old's methamphetamine overdose was no accident. According to the coroner's report, Alex's body contained nearly nineteen times the lethal limit of meth. The teen's family and friends believe he was murdered with a hot shot to ensure silence about what he had learned of the West Point meth world. Crabtree has felt a dogged loyalty to examining every lead in that direction, even carrying a photograph of Alex with him as he's confronted numerous addicts who might have information.

On July 26, Crabtree was investigating a burglary in Railroad Flat when one of the suspects in the break-in, 55-year-old Neil Goddard, cruised by on a motorcycle. Crabtree had already scored a warrant for Goddard. He jumped into a newly issued undercover Ford F250, activated hidden patrol lights and slammed his foot on the gas. The hot wail of its siren slung through the pines. Goddard looked over his shoulder and revved the Harley's engine. The detective's hands tightened on his steering wheel in response. In a half-second, the motorcycle burned down a shady, wooded lane—almost out of sight—heading toward the same barn where the crazed mountain man had ambushed Calaveras Sheriff's deputies six months before. Crabtree felt the wheels of the F250 battling gravity through windy, fast-coming curves. The pursuit whirled by a crew of phone company workers, who cheered the sheriff's department truck as it sped by. All at once, Goddard found himself accelerating into an unexpected intersection at Upper June Avenue. He lost control of the Harley and crashed into a shallow embankment. Crabtree rode his truck's brakes, trying not to plow over his own suspect. The detective broke out of the cab with his .40 caliber training up on the wreckage. "Neil, get your hands where I can see them!" Crabtree yelled.

Goddard lay bleeding under the dusty, steel anchor of the Harley. "Hands!" Crabtree repeated. Pinned down, Goddard could only manage to fumble his left arm up. Crabtree was already on top of him, realizing that Goddard had a loaded pistol in his waistband and a baggie of meth in his pocket.

As Crabtree took his suspect into custody, trying not to let blood get smeared on himself, the only resident who walked outside to make sure he was all right was Katie Anderson, Alex Anderson's mother.

Crabtree took his wife Tammie out to dinner the following evening. They were seated by a window that looked out on the rustic gables of Main Street, Sutter Creek. Josh drank a tall Sierra Nevada. Tammie sipped on a glass of wine. They quietly discussed the pursuit with Goddard and other white-knuckled encounters Josh had been involved in since his standoff with the Hells Angels in summer of 2010. For Tammie's part, her work at the women's safe house may not grab newspaper headlines, but the feats of emotional strength and unconditional compassion she and her fellow advocates summon every day are challenges few can relate to. In June of 2011, Tammie met "Heather," a meth-addict prostitute legitimately fearing for her life. Heather revealed she has been beaten and raped numerous times while feeding her addiction, and the most recent danger was coming from a meth-dealer boyfriend who threatened to beat her to death for not participating in group-sex acts. It's a disturbing report, but Heather admits her addiction has leveled far greater amounts of pain on others than herself: All four of her children have been taken away from her by child protective services. Heather's second son was born with major birth defects, rendered wheelchair-bound and severely disabled for life because of his mother's rampant drug use. Having raised two daughters, this part of Heather's story leaves Tammie—as well as the other mothers at the safe house—speechless. In a different place and time, it would be Heather's children Tammie and her co-workers would be fighting to rescue. But those children are protected. They have been for a long time. Now there was only Heather, alone in the world, without a job, without a home, without teeth, and afraid she would be dead soon if she was not protected. Bound to honor the rights and dignity of every client looking for help, Tammie did everything she could to navigate Heather through the court system and get the support she needed.

CALAVERAS COUNTY sheriff's deputies Kevin Stevens and Josh Shemensky made full recoveries from their gunfight along the muddy slopes near West Point. Both were awarded a special commendation, along with Sgt. Dave Seawell, who had raced to their aid, and every member of the Calaveras sheriff's SWAT that had surrounded and captured Richard Kenneth Cooper.

Between January and May of 2011, Cooper's public defender attempted to cope with the overwhelming evidence mounting against his client. There were numerous items of physical evidence, from the pill bottle inside the "mountain man's" car with Cooper's name on it, to the 12-gauge shotgun recovered inside Stephen Grommringer's house, to the ammunition grabbed from Cooper's pocket as he was being handcuffed, to statements directly from Cooper's mouth to law enforcement. Even more problematic for Cooper's attorney was the fact that Stevens and Shemensky had been nine feet away from the mountain man during the ambush, and both positively identified Richard Kenneth Cooper as the man who had tried to murder them.

Cooper's first trial was scheduled for June of 2011. Weeks before it began, his attorney convinced a judge that more investigation was needed from the public defender's office, as well as new and lengthy expert consultation. The trial was re-scheduled for September of that year. Several days before jury selection got underway, Cooper's attorney filed a 1368 motion with the court, which, in the jargon of the California legal system, amounted to a challenge to his client's mental competence to stand trial. This move by the defense caught law enforcement and observers by surprise. Despite Cooper's documented history and known reputation for firing methamphetamine with needles, he'd appeared lucid, even keenly alert, throughout his series of court appearances. Now his attorney was telling reporters—after representing Cooper for nearly nine months—that he was suddenly concerned about whether his client really understood what was going on inside the courtroom. The defense also implied that it would hold contested hearings even if the doctors ordered to examine Cooper's mental state issued opinions that the 54-year-old was indeed competent.

As of this writing, Cooper has not stood trial for the charge of attempted murder.

One man who eventually did face his day in court was Victor Callahan, charged with killing Ysauro Lujan with his vehicle in the summer of 2009. Callahan's prosecution was slow and methodical, but ultimately the People's strategy of charging him with second-degree murder paid off. Amador County District Attorney Todd Riebe and prosecutor Steve Hermanson knew they could prove Callahan had substantial amounts of methamphetamine in his system when he veered into the Lujans. Coupled with a highly detailed death scene investigation from the California Highway Patrol, the blood evidence could likely get a jury to call Ysauro's death an act of murder. Callahan's public defender made him see that the best course of action would be to take a plea bargain in which he admitted guilt to the lesser charge of gross vehicular manslaughter. On November 24, 2010, Callahan was sentenced to fourteen years in state prison without possibility of early release. The deal was engineered primarily by Hermanson, who also made an offer to the same public defender in the case of Roger Lamarra, the suspected Peckerwood gang member who had been caught by Chris Rice transporting methamphetamine through Jackson. Lamarra pled guilty to felony possession and was sentenced to five years in prison without possibility of early release. During his sentencing, Lamarra told Judge David Richmond that he sincerely wanted treatment for his methamphetamine addiction.

For Riebe, an avid newspaper reader, 2010 was marked by a series of bizarre headlines that continued well into 2011. It started in July of 2010, when California Highway Patrol officer Ruben Salago was arrested for possession of methamphetamine, driving under the influence of methamphetamine and attempting to hire a hit man to murder a meth-addict witness planning to testify against him for buying the drug. Disgraced, Salago eventually pled guilty to the charges in a Placer County courtroom. He was sentenced to three years in state prison. In April of 2011, *The New York Times* ran a story about Tommy

Adams, a young man elected Sheriff of Carter County in Missouri. Adams's jurisdiction fell over a span of the Ozark Mountains with fewer than seven thousand residents. Adams was eventually arrested for using methamphetamine and selling it around the various regions of the county. The headlines continued. Riebe watched each story grow harder to believe than the last. In June, 2011 the *Associated Press* syndicated a story entitled, "Woman to Stand Trial in Meth Breast Milk Death." The piece told the story of Maggie Wortman of Humboldt County, California, who was being held to answer for the death of her newborn son, Michael, after the infant's body tested positive for significant amounts of methamphetamine that could have only come from "meth-laced breast milk." Humboldt County Deputy District Attorney Ben McLaughlin alleged that Wortman's 19-month old daughter also tested positive for having methamphetamine in her system. Wortman's story was followed by another disturbing news piece in September of 2011. *Reuters news* reported that a kindergartner in rural Sweet Springs, Missouri, took a glass pipe and bag of crystal methamphetamine to school for show-and-tell. The boy's 32-year-old mother was arrested on drug charges and held without bail.

Toward the end of 2011, the American Society of Addiction Medicine issued a press release to media across the United States announcing it had formulated a new definition for the term addiction. According to the ASAM, addiction should now be defined as a chronic brain disorder, and not as problematic choices or behaviors. "Many behaviors driven by addiction are real problems and sometimes criminal acts," Doctor Michael Miller conceded in the release. "But the disease is about brains, not drugs. It's about underlying neurology, not outward actions."

Almost as soon as the definition was unveiled, Maia Szalavitz, a health journalist for TIME Magazine, wrote about some of its flaws. Szalavitz pointed out that data indicates a majority of individuals diagnosed with various addictions actually recover on their own "without treatment or participation in self-help groups," causing problematic comparisons with established brain disorders like schizophrenia, epilepsy and Alzheimer's disease. Szalavitz also predicted that, by linking addiction to major brain disease and permanent brain impairments, the ASAM was actually increasing the stigma around addiction, rather than softening it. Various addiction counselors and commentators writing on the blogosphere were also highly critical of the ASAM's definition.

For Todd Riebe, social debates raging around why his court calendar remains full do little to help with the immediate problems of coping with tremendous caseloads, a dwindling budget and a crippling lack of space in the Amador County Jail. Besides, most rural county prosecutors would note that the ASAM's decision to lump all forms of addictions into one all-encompassing category only obfuscates the real question dominating the open countryside of America: Why methamphetamine? How can one synthetic compound hold a stranglehold on diverse rural communities across the nation that cocaine, crack, heroine, Oxycontin and even alcohol fail to match, fail to supplant, fail to penetrate? And, if all addictions are the same, as the ASAM purports, how has methamphetamine alone become the force that threatens to put the criminal justice system in America's mountains, ranchlands and farmlands on its knees? The ASAM's view that all addictions are essentially the same also seems to dismiss first-hand testimonials from addicts like "Kelly," who says that only methamphetamine could help her escape the buried pain of being abused and molested as a child; or "Betty," who used meth as a way of coping with a long-shattered self-esteem. The definition also does little to explain how a person like Matthew Learned could easily juggle marijuana, alcohol and cocaine—only to watch his life dive into a 30-year tailspin after encountering methamphetamine. Nor does it account for why, after more than 30 years of practicing law, Superior Court Judge David Richmond refers to meth as "the worst drug ever unleashed on Man."

Despite the lack of answers, Riebe does what he can to stay informed about medical and psychiatric data on methamphetamine. He has been open to clinic evaluations of the drug's power before. Riebe's most disturbing case from his time as a public defender remains that of Grover Graham, the man who murdered his infant daughter with a pair of scissors and then tried to bludgeon his wife to death—all while being tormented by meth-conjured hallucinations. It was Riebe who had turned to doctors to explore why a man with no history of violence had committed one of the most heinous acts that law enforcement in Madera County could remember. Grover's eventual diagnosis of amphetamine-induced psychotic disorder allowed for him to be committed to Napa State Hospital for an undetermined amount of time rather than spending life in prison. Riebe hoped significant medical intervention might help Grover cope with what he had done and someday find a way back to mental and moral clarity.

In 1994, Robert Lewis, the truck driver who had stopped Grover from killing his wife, Maria Graham, was awarded numerous commendations and named a citizen hero by the Madera

County Sheriff's Office. Years passed. Grover's crime began to fade from public memory. But the crime did not fade for Lewis. He had arrived at that bloody spot on the freeway in time to fight Grover and prevent him from ending Maria's life, but it was still too late to save little Candice. He thought about the murdered baby for years. A career trucker, Lewis was required to travel from southern to northern California on a weekly basis; but he would do almost anything to avoid passing that stretch of State Route 99 where the child had been killed. Lewis eventually dealt with the crime on his own terms, mostly by focusing on his wife, children and grandchildren. He never lost his signature sense of humor or the enjoyment he got from having fun with family and friends. Robert Lewis passed away in 2009.

Grover Graham was released from Napa State Hospital in 2003. Given the fact that his diagnosis was dependent on having psychotic episodes from methamphetamine use, after seven years in a hospital, with no access to meth, doctors had limited justification to hold him. Grover walked out to freedom on an early March afternoon. In December of 2008, he was arrested by the Fresno Police Department for possession of a controlled substance. Grover's new charges were ultimately dismissed after a judge ruled to suppress a key piece of evidence in the case; but by that time state correctional investigators had already determined that Grover had been buying illegal drugs, was involved in the drug world and "posed a dangerous threat to the health and safety of others," including his new children. Grover was re-incarcerated in Napa State Hospital in 2009, the same year Robert Lewis, the man who had stopped him from committing a double-homicide, died.

None of this recent history was known to Todd Riebe, who

spent most of 2009 and 2010 overseeing the prosecution of an internationally monitored homicide case in Amador County, as well as the second-degree murder case against Victor Callahan. On a summer morning in 2010, Riebe was waiting alone in the hallway of a courthouse when he ran into the crime journalist who had been following up on Grover. "He was actually released several years ago," the reporter told him. "But then he was arrested again on new drug charges."

For an instant, Riebe was completely silent. "Are you serious?" he whispered. "After all of that?"

The district attorney still sees the face of Grover Graham.

AUTHOR'S NOTE

HENRY L. LUCE, the founder of TIME Magazine, once reflected, "I became a journalist to come as close as possible to the heart of the world." With an eye to the impact, commitment and sacrifice of those writers who have gone before me, this book is meant to be an authentic and uncompromising work of journalism. Its stories are real. The names of the law enforcement officers, the attorneys, the victims' advocates, the experts, the citizens and the citizen heroes within its pages are their true names. Nearly all convicted criminals, drug offenders and meth addicts are also identified by their actual names, though in a handful of instances in Chapter 3, the names of a few were amended to a first name only, or amended to a first and middle name only, in order to protect the identities of young children that are named victims in criminal abuse and neglect investigations. As is typical of crime journalism, some adult victims of violent crimes, specifically in Chapter 7, are not identified by their names to protect their future safety. The use of monikers in several cases—such as "Jack," or "The Kid"—were necessary to protect the lives of various individuals who have been witnesses in murder cases, or attempted murder cases.

The process of writing this book began in April of 2010, when a major grant from the Phillips Foundation provided me with funding to study the relationship between crime and methamphetamine addiction in rural parts of the United States. In the years leading up to that, my work as a crime reporter in California gave me a front-row seat to the untold story of meth in America, a saga of families being destroyed, children being abused and the rise of unchecked crime. The initial grant from the Phillips Foundation allowed for a probe of rural America's meth problem on a level that would have been otherwise out of reach: It has enabled me to spend eighteen months—between May of 2010 and October of 2011—embedded part-time with rural county law enforcement agencies in northern California. My work included partnering with officers on night patrols, accompanying detectives on warrant searches and probation sweeps, observing SWAT operations and spending hundreds of hours with attorneys and victims' advocates in small-town courtrooms.

The Phillips Foundation also provided me with funds to travel to different rural communities across the United States to study how methamphetamine is threatening these essential pieces of America.

Tackling a subject as endemic as meth was a major challenge. I don't think I would have had a clue where to start without the inspiration of three particular figures: The World War II correspondent Ernie Pyle, the master literary journalist, Jon Franklin, and Baltimore's David Simon, whose books "Homicide" and "The Corner" represent some of the finest domestic reporting I've ever encountered. In keeping with the tradition of these journalists and many others, the bulk present-tense narratives in *Shadow People*—contained in chapters 1, 3, 5, 7, 9, and the epilogue—are events that I witnessed first-hand while embedded with law enforcement officers. These same chapters also contain a few pieces of action that I didn't witness, though in each case I was embedded with other officers in the general area, and was fully briefed within hours, if not minutes, of the incident happening. In contrast, the book's descriptions of crimes that occurred in the past, such as the murder of Candice Graham or the murder Travis Hoppola, are based on exhaustive reconstruction, which required poring through police reports, superior court records, court transcripts, newspaper clippings and, most importantly, extensive interviews with witnesses, investigators and individuals familiar with those crimes.

During the 900 hours I spent embedded with law enforcement agencies, I always wore a press badge around my neck. I wanted any suspect being confronted or arrested to know that a professional journalist was present. But few suspects bothered to read my badge. Most glanced at it and assumed I was an undercover investigator, a police cadet or a county health official. Given the frequency of these identification issues, I started making sure that any meth addict or dealer who struck up a meaningful conversation with me understood that I was a journalist, and that I was working on a major media project.

The research for *Shadow People* began at a time when trust between law enforcement and the media had arguably never been worse. Given that, I was concerned that police chiefs and county sheriffs would be reluctant to give me significant access to the reality of what their officers see when it comes to methamphetamine. I had some help with the sales pitch from Amador County Sheriff Martin Ryan and Jackson Police Chief Scott Morrison. Both men were the first to open their agencies up to me for long-term, serious embedded work. For Ryan, the move was part of a much larger public awareness battle he had fought all that year against methamphetamine in the corridors of California's state capital. Ryan had teamed up with Alyson Huber, a democratic assemblywoman whose tenth district covers much of the region described in the present-tense narratives of this book, to pass Assembly Bill 640, which aimed to give methamphetamine dealers the same amount of jail time as cocaine, crack and heroin dealers. "Methamphetamine use is at a crisis point in the state," Huber told her fellow California legislators, "and it's at a crisis point in my own district." With bi-partisan support from Republican sheriffs like Ryan—a former Bureau Chief for the California Attorney General's Office and former head of California state intelligence— as well as then-Sacramento County Sheriff John McGinness, Huber pulled off a legislative miracle: She convinced California Democrats and Republicans to vote unanimously on the same bill. The legislation was ultimately vetoed by out-going Governor Arnold Swargzenegger; though Martin Ryan continued to speak out about the tremendous level of crime methamphetamine was spawning in his county and its ever-present connection to elder abuse and child abuse.

Jackson Police Chief Scott Morrison was the law enforcement administrator I knew best from my work as a crime reporter. A strong believer in public transparency, Morrison ultimately gave me an incredible amount of access to his night patrols, narcotics operations, special details and drug investigations. I am convinced having the immediate cooperation of Martin Ryan and Scott Morrison was a vote of confidence that helped open doors for me at other law enforcement agencies. Morrison also pointed me in the direction of his brother, Lance Morrison, a nationally recognized expert on methamphetamine, and a man whose help was vital to the creation of this book.

Lance Morrison, and his Sergeant at the Oakley Police Department, Robert Roberts, allowed me to accompany an outstanding group of officers on night patrols, from the edges of Antioch to the waters of Bethel Island. Around the same time Ione Police Chief Mike Johnson and a number of captains and sergeants at the Calaveras County Sheriff's Department were granting me access to patrols, warrant searches and a host of ongoing investigations. In January of 2011, the top narcotics detective for the Amador County District Attorney's Office, John D'Agostini, was elected sheriff of neighboring El Dorado County. D'Agostini's former boss, Todd Riebe, was a steadfast supporter of this book and once D'Agostini took the helm in El Dorado, he opened his agency up to me for being embedded on night patrols. I owe a special thanks to Lieutenant Robert Ashworth for helping coordinate my research and patrols.

Any police officer, sheriff's deputy or detective whose name appears in this book did so by permission. Some, like Jackson Police detective Chris Rice, simply asked that it be made clear he worked very closely with other investigators on most of the cases mentioned in my narratives, particularly Amador County sheriff's detectives Justin Colletti and Cameron Begbie, Sutter Creek police detective Tizok De Rio and California highway patrol narcotics detective Brandon Hallam.

For me, the most important thing for readers to understand is that the names of some of the officers I spent the most time with during those eighteen months never appear within the pages of this book. The mission to make *Shadow People* a national study complete with glimpses of the American West, Mid West and the deep South required omitting literally hundreds of arrests and investigations I observed in my journey as an embedded reporter. While the names and distinct personalities of those officers did not make it into my published narrative, they're nonetheless the invisible backbone of whatever success this book has in bringing awareness to the connection between methamphetamine addiction and crimes against the innocent. The book would not have been possible without these men and women. The individuals who weren't mentioned that I'm most indebted to are Jose Arevalos, Al Lewis, Chris Mynderup and Christy Stidger of the Jackson Police Department; Chris Crandell, John FooSum, Jeremy Martin, Greg Moon, Brandon Kohn, Patrick Wert and Gary Redman of the Amador County Sheriff's Office; Rocky Harpham and Pollie Pent of the Ione Police Department, Dave Seawell and Greg Stark of the Calaveras County Sheriff's Department; Lance Bryant, Russ Adams, James Hubert and John Densmore of the El Dorado County Sheriff's Office; and Scott Taylor and F. Pullido of the Sonora Office of the California Highway Patrol.

A few of the officers mentioned above, like Arevalos, Mynderup, Lewis, Crandell and FooSum—and nearly all of the officers and detectives mentioned within the book's narratives—spent countless hours with me over the course of seven changes in the seasons. They watched my back. They kept me safe. They let me stand by them when suspect confrontations got tense. They traded jokes with me inside of hospital emergency rooms. They had coffee with me at two in the morning in gas stations. They made this project real.

On April 18, 1945 war journalist Ernie Pyle was killed by Japanese machine-gunners while he was embedded with U.S. troops in Okinawa. It was the closing days of World War II and Germany had just surrendered. Inside the dead reporter's pocket was his last newspaper column, which focused largely on the American troops he had spent more than two years embedded with in Italy as they fought the German war machine: "Now I am as far away from it as possible … but my heart is still in Europe, and that is why I am writing this column. It is to the boys who were my friends for so long. My one regret of the war is that I was not with them when it ended."

For the peace officers I mentioned above, it never "ends." And my one regret is that I won't be with them to see the future victories, like arresting a violent fugitive stalking through a peaceful county neighborhood, or snapping a pair of handcuffs on a so-called man who's pummeled his girlfriend's face to sickening colors, or carrying a small, underfed child who's covered in dirt and flea bites out of a meth house. Finite victories. Silent victories. Anonymous and mostly forgotten victories. But victories nonetheless.

—Scott Thomas Anderson
Washington D.C.
October, 2011